WINNING ARCHERY

WINNING ARCHERY

by **Steve Ruis**

Editor of Archery Focus Magazine

WATCHING ARROWS FLY, LLC

Library of Congress Cataloging-in Publication Data

Winning Archery / Steve Ruis.
    p. cm
    Includes bibliographic references and index.
    ISBN 978-0-9821471-5-3 (softcover)
    1. Archery. 2. Training I Steve Ruis, 1946-

ISBN: 978-0-9821471-6-0

The web addresses cited in this text were current as of June 2012, unless otherwise noted.

Writer: Steve Ruis; **Copy Editor**; Steve Ruis; **Proofreader**: Claudia Stevenson; **Graphic Artist**: Steve Ruis; **Cover Designer**: Steve Ruis; **Photographers** (cover and interior): Steve Ruis and Claudia Stevenson unless otherwise noted; **Illustrator** Steve Ruis

Printed in the United States of America 10 9 8 7 6 5 4 3 2 1

Watching Arrows Fly
3712 North Broadway, #285
Chicago, IL 60613
800. 671.1140

Dedication

He might not know it but much of the material in this book came from me trying to figure out how my best friend and mentor (and many time national champion and record holder) Rusty Mills kept winning and winning and winning. . . . Thanks, Rusty!

Steve Ruis
June 2012

Contents

Preface

Do You Want to Learn How to Win?

Since you are reading this, it is at least somewhat clear that you are interested in winning archery competitions. But every eight-year old who gives archery a try wants to win, so how do you know that you really want to learn how to win? An answer to this question is fairly simple:

1.   You have learned something about archery (enough to enter a competition).
2.   You did fairly well at a competition (at least enjoyed yourself), and
3.   You had the thought "You know, if I worked at this I could get pretty good and could win a competition like this . . ." (or something similar).
     "That's it?" you ask.

Well, this is the typical starting point in the development of a winning archer. You may be relatively inexperienced at archery or you may have been in the sport for years, but now having tasted the possibilities, you want to learn how to win.

I expect there are three broad classes of archers who will benefit from this book:

#1
Archers who are just starting to compete who
want to get a head start on learning how to win.

#2
Archers who have been competing for a year or so and
are frustrated they are not making more progress.

#3
Archers who have competed for quite a while but
never seem to get to those top three spots.

The more experience you have, the more you will be skipping over parts of this book because you have already learned them, but since you do not know what it is you are looking for, I suggest you skim those parts you are inclined to skip in case they aren't what you thought they were.

The vast majority of archers believe that winning archery tournaments involves merely learning how to shoot well. This belief is bolstered by the fact that the vast majority of archery books on the market (including our book, *Precision Archery*) are about learning to shoot well or, at least, to shoot better. Unfortunately this is only about half of the task. Ask any competing archer for funny competition stories and you will get stories of archers who showed up at a six arrow shoot with five arrows, archers who forgot to bring their bow sight, archers who showed up at a competition without their arrows (or their bow) but with everything else, archer's whose luggage (clothes and archery gear) was lost by an airline, archers who were disqualified because they were wearing the wrong clothes (Yes, some organizations have dress codes.), archers who lost or were disqualified because of rules violations, archers who got lost on the way to the competition range and were scratched, archers who ate something that gave them food poisoning and knocked them out of the competition, archers who could not afford to attend a major competition, archers who could not get leave from the military to attend the Olympic archery trials, archers . . . need I go on? And, by the way, these are all true stories. (One of them happened to me.)

There is a tremendous amount of information that needs to be gathered, plans that need to be made, rules that need to be learned, practices that need to be followed, and people who need to be involved and none of these involve shooting arrows well.

Unfortunately, you will also get stories from other archers about how seemingly easy it is to start winning. They will tell you stories of archers they knew (or knew of) who won from the beginning and won often, so it can't be that hard, can it? Again, unfortunately, they may tell you a story about a "natural" archer who won competitions from the start, but they won't tell you about the hundreds of other archers they have known who not only didn't win from the start, they ended up giving up along the way due to frustration.

You see, you can't really know you want to learn to be a winning archer until you know what it takes to become one.

This is what this book is about.

Here are all of the things that make archers into winners in one place, so you can decide whether you want to be one of them. Also, if you do take the plunge, this book is a prescription for success and winning in archery. You will learn all of the things you won't get from the other books and you will learn quite a bit about how to learn to shoot well, too. Avoiding many of the common pitfalls can make your path to the winner's platform smoother.

Steve Ruis
Chicago
June 2012

1

The Elements of Winning Archery

"Golf is the only sport where the most feared opponent is yourself."
Anonymous
"Oh, and Archery, too!"
Steve Ruis

Shooting arrows well an absolutely necessary skill needed to win archery tournaments, but too many archers think it is the *only* thing needed in learning to win tournaments and they couldn't be more wrong. There are a great many other aspects of winning besides shooting well that are required to win consistently. In this chapter I will lay out for you all of the elements of winning archery. Then in the subsequent chapters we will look at each of these elements in detail.

Talent

I start with something you don't need—talent.

"Huh, but. . . ."

I know, I know, you've heard it your whole life: this athlete or that athlete is "a natural talent" or has "God-given talent." Well, for many decades scientists have been trying to identify what a "talent" is and so far they have come up with exactly nothing; in fact, it looks as if they won't. Accept it now, there is no such thing as "talent." This doesn't mean that people don't learn certain things more easily than others or that we all aren't much better at certain tasks than others. The point is that it isn't because of some specific talent for painting or violin playing or chess or math or sports that we can do so. That probably does not exist.

When people talk about an athlete's "talent" they are usually referring to the quality of that athlete's performance, based upon countless hours of practice, not on some innate genetic ability. What people do have is abilities or attributes. If you are a basketball player and you are tall it helps; if you are very tall, it helps a great deal. But if you are simultaneously tall and very clumsy, you probably will not get very far in basketball. To be a good baseball player you need great hand-eye coor-

3

dination, not so much to be a football offensive lineman, but there it helps if you are tall and strong and quick, but not necessarily fast. Many of these attributes can be enhanced: you can become faster, stronger, or quicker through training, although we all have limits (which are largely genetic). Nobody has figured a way to train people to be taller, for example. These attributes contribute to the possibilities of success. The number of tennis players, good male tennis players, under 5´8˝ or over 6´6˝ are very, very few. But the majority of professional basketball players are over 6´6˝. This has nothing to do with "talent."

So, if one doesn't need talent, what does one need? Well, to shoot well you have to be calm and focused, so those qualities are nice, but they can also be learned. You need to not be easily discouraged. If you find a limit to your abilities, it helps if it motivates you to find a way beyond that limit, rather than discourages you. Basically, if you want to become a winning archer, you have to have a passion for practice; you have to like to practice. If you have the physical attributes for a sport (and most people do for archery), it takes a great deal of effort and practice to reach the top. If you don't enjoy the work, you probably won't stick it out long enough to get good enough to win.

I have a definition for being an "adult," it goes like this: adults can enjoy hard work. I have known 14-year old adults and 45-year old kids by my definition. If you don't enjoy the work associated with practicing, that is you don't address it in an adult manner, you will not make it.

So, why does the concept of "talent" exist if there isn't such a thing? My guess is it stems from ego protection. Right after some guy beats your brains out on the archery field, who wants to admit that the other guy simply trained harder, or tried harder, or just made fewer mistakes. It salves the ego to think that they had some genetic or "God-given" talent that you weren't given, so losing doesn't hurt so much.

Assessing Where You Are (Chapter 2)

Part of getting where you want to go is knowing where you are now. Part of the process of getting better is having some indication that what you are doing is working. To know these things you have to be able to assess "where you are" in your archery skills. If you were working diligently on something and you were getting worse, would you keep doing it? What if what you are doing to assess "where you are" is giving you incorrect information?

In this chapter I will suggest things you can do to assess your progress and establish where you are. Actually this is a recurring theme throughout this book. You will find mention of, and techniques for, assessing yourself in more than just this chapter. That's because assessment is critical for you to make progress and meet your goals.

Winning Equipment (Chapter 3)

A winning archer needs the very best equipment, right? Top of the line bow

($1000+), bow sight ($300-500), stabilizer system ($200-350), arrows ($200-400), etc. This would be a good place to start, right?

Er, ah, *no*. In fact such equipment, before you are ready to take advantage of it, can be detrimental to your development. (Top flight equipment can be very sensitive as to how well it is handled.)

I can hear the disappointment sighing from every young archer reading this, their dreams of beautiful archery gear flying off on gossamer wings. But, it is true: you do not need top of the line equipment to become a top flight archer. What you need is adequate equipment, which is equipment that is good enough and which has been carefully fitted to you. "Adequate" is defined as "not limiting your performance." As long as you are getting good feedback from the target, you can get better. Good feedback means the positions of the arrows landing on the target are determined by what you have done and not by your equipment. Bent arrows, for example, don't give good feedback. Straight arrows can.

To ensure your equipment is "adequate" you will need help, some from Chapter 3 and some you will have to secure in the makeup of your support team.

Oh, and don't worry—if you earn it, you will have all of that top notch equipment to shoot.

Winning Technique (Chapter 4)

I could tell you stories of self-made champions, but they would be stories from half a century, or longer, ago. The level of competition is such that one really can't do it alone any more. You need contributions from specialists. Particularly troubling with regard to archery technique is that "the experts" are still debating most aspects of it.

Technique in archery consists of two parts: form (also called posture) and execution. I would be hard pressed to address any aspect of archery technique without mentioning that there is more than one recommendation regarding it.

The good news is that the differences being debated may not count for much. The 2008 men's Olympic archery champion, Viktor Ruban of Ukraine, won his gold medal while exhibiting two common "form flaws," which are things almost every coach would tell you not to do. Those two practices may not be optimal, but they certainly didn't cost Mr. Ruban an Olympic gold medal.

We will look at this in some detail. I say only "some" detail, because this is the topic of most target archery books, so the literature is extensive.

The bottom line is you will probably need help from a good coach to refine your technique.

Winning Physical Training (Chapter 5)

There are people who insist on breaking down issues along the lines of "there are two kinds of . . . " followed by their favorite dichotomy (people who like dogs and people who like cats, or people who believe in God and people who don't, etc.). I am not one of those, but . . . in archery there are two kinds of competitors, those who do physical training and those who don't.

Do those who do have an edge?

The answer is a resounding ... maybe.

You have to be very careful when asking people about this topic. As I am writing this chapter the 2010 Winter Olympics is under way and there are stories everywhere about the training elite athletes will engage in to get an edge on their competitors. Many of these activities are attempts to get another one percent or even a fraction of one percent better performance. You will need to figure out just how much advantage such efforts provide to wisely decide on whether you want to embark on a physical training regimen. Then you need to know what kinds of physical training are useful. For example, will jogging help your archery? The answer: probably not (besides there are much more effective ways to provide the cardiovascular fitness archers need).

We will discuss this whole topic and suggest ways for you to decide whether you need a physical training plan and, if so, suggest good resources to you.

Winning Mental Training (Chapter 6)

I am just returned from the 2010 World Archery Festival as I write this and I recall that a former champion, Chance Beaubouef, when asked what his greatest asset was replied: "a strong mental program." Huh, a guy wins $25,000 and he doesn't think it is his bow, or his sterling technique, or wants to give his coach props? It's his "mental game?"

Yep.

There is a joke in archery on this topic; it goes like this:

Me Winning scores, even perfect scores are easy!

You Really?

Me Yes, it is a simple two step process:

Step 1 Shoot a bull's-eye.

Step 2 Repeat Step 1 as necessary.

Even non-archers find this amusing because everyone recognizes the apparent silliness of it, the problem being in the word "repeat;" it is not so simple. Yet, a great many archers design their practice based on this "principle." They go to an archery range and shoot arrows for X hours. (Oh, a good one! Oh, missed that time. Oh, darn, another miss., etc.) Supposedly, if they shoot long enough, they will string together a series of good shots and feel like they have accomplished something. In reality very little has been accomplished.

Elite archers are thinking their way from shot to shot and through each shot. (That shot was low. Why was it low? Maybe I need to focus on holding my bow up during followthrough. Let's try that. Oh, back on center, good!) The thinking while making the shot is largely subconscious while the thinking between shots is largely conscious, but thinking from shot to shot is necessary because it is physically impossible to shoot two shots the exact same way. What has to happen is small adjustments made continually to maintain a high level of accuracy and consistency. One's mental program consists of all the things one does mentally to keep on track or to get back on track if you get off of it.

In this chapter, we will sketch out what is needed (including how to deal with head games and trash talking) and point you to all of the best sources of mental training.

Winning Practice (Chapter 7)

The subject of what to do while practicing comes up in every one of the other chapters, but here I will provide some of the critical aspects of practicing that winners need to know.

Planning to Win (Chapter 8)

Most beginning competitive archers think that all they need to do is to learn to shoot well and they are in the money. I hope by now that you realize that this is wrong. Part of learning how to win is getting experience winning which requires you to win to learn how to win! Learning how to win also includes you taking charge of all of the things that can affect your performance, most of which have nothing to do with shooting.

You do not want to learn these lessons the hard way. For example, I once got to a competition and set up my bow, arrows, quiver, etc. I had my tools with me as well as having packed a lunch, but unfortunately my bow sight was at home, sitting on my workbench. End of tournament. Ask any archer about competing and they will have at least one story that is similar (showing up without bow, arrows, release aid, membership documents, tab, etc.). Archers will also have stories about flying to a tournament and having their luggage (and bow, arrows, etc.) lost by the airline.

In addition to being responsible for your logistics, you need to know whether you have any chance of winning. The only way to do this is to keep records. For example, a competition you would like to win had a winning score of 286/300 last year (and similar scores the previous few years). If your average practice score on that round is 286, then you have about a 50% chance of winning (half of the time your score is higher, half the time it is lower). Well, you would have a 50% chance of winning if your competition scores are similar to your practice scores . . . and if the same people show up who showed up last year and if they haven't gotten much better, and. . . . I think you get the point. If you only have some vague desire to win, you are really just wishing or hoping. If you have solid evidence recorded that you can shoot a winning score, then you have a good reason to believe you will be at or near the top in a competition. Which of these situations would make you more confident, do you think? And you do know that confidence in your abilities is good for your performance, yes?

And . . . you will need plans for training, plans for competing, plans for raising funds if your travel expenses exceed your resources, etc.

You will need plans. The nice thing is you don't have to do all of the work yourself as you will have people supporting your efforts who can help you. And you will have Chapter 8, too!

Developing Your Support Team (Chapter 9)

Archery is mostly an individual sport. When you imagine yourself on the medal stand, you don't think of yourself standing with teammates, but make no mistake there will be a team of people helping you. Whoever first said, "It takes a village to raise a child," got it right, and it also takes a team a create a winning athlete.

If you are young, typically your parents are your core team; if you are married, your spouse is automatically part of your team—whether they participate or not! Anyone trying to achieve excellence in any field ends up shirking the common duties they would do if they weren't pursuing that level of excellence. Other people end up shopping for groceries, mowing the lawn, washing the dishes, etc. while you are practicing and competing. Parents and spouses go without so you can afford better equipment, travel, and tournament fees.

You are also going to need technical expertise from coaches, bow mechanics, physical trainers, and mental skills experts, among others. These people have to be chosen with care, fired when needs be, and usually paid for what they do for you.

Chapter 9 will give you a head start on developing (and learning to appreciate) your team.

Competing to Win (Chapter 10)

After you have done all of the training, taken care of your logistics, you are good to go to a tournament and win. Well, maybe. There is much you can do once you get there to make sure you have the best chance of performing well.

Every successful athlete has competition routines to support what they are doing. These routines cover warm-up, snacks, breaks, getting to and back from the venue, sightseeing, and more. By the time you are through with this chapter, you will know what to do.

Navigating the Archery Organizations (Chapter 11)

Before you get to even sniff the air at the shooting line of a major archery competition, you will learn that archery competitions aren't put on just for the heck of it. Behind every competition is a sponsoring archery organization. Since each of these organizations wants to continue to exist, they require all competitors to be members of their organization to compete for medals and prizes.

Oh, you can shoot in almost all archery competitions as a "guest," but you will not win, get a trophy or medal, or possibly even get your score posted. Organizations who allowed archers to compete and not be members would quickly no longer exist.

So, which organizations should you join? What does membership entail? What do you need to know to avoid making costly mistakes in competition?

These are all good questions. For one, all of these organizations have their own rules, often their own targets, scoring schemes, and traditions. In one organization, if you turn in an incorrect score card, you are disqualified; in another, if you turn in an incorrect scorecard you may be penalized (if you turn in a higher score than you shot it will be corrected downward; if a lower score, you are stuck with the lower score).

I will lead you though the maze and give you tips and suggestions about how to avoid most of the mistakes (and the politics).

Competing Internationally (Chapter 12)

Archery is taken much more seriously overseas than it is here in the U.S. If you compete overseas, there is a whole new set of issues that you need to be aware of and be able to deal with. But, don't worry, we have your back.

Questions and Answers (Chapter 13)

(Like it says.)

Any time you are ready to start, all you have to do is turn the page. Whether you actually win, of course, depends upon your performance. Your performance depends a great deal on your attitude and on who you are. If you can master yourself, you can master your performance and you can win.
Enjoy the process!

Key Points
Chapter 1 The Elements of Winning Archery

This chapter is an overview of the chapters to come, so most of the key points alluded to will be found in those other chapters.

- You don't need talent to be a winning archer.
- To shoot well you must be calm and focused under the tension of the drawn bow. Relaxation is key.
- If you find a limit to your abilities, it helps if it motivates you to find a way beyond that limit, rather than discourages you.
- To become a winning archer, you have to have a passion for practice; you have to *like* to practice.
- Part of the process of getting better is having some indication that what you are doing is working.
- Top-of-the-line equipment, before you are ready to take advantage of it, can be detrimental to your development.
- Archers who do physical training have an edge . . . maybe.
- Elite archers are thinking their way from shot to shot and through each shot.
- It is preferred to not learn everything "the hard way."
- If you only have some vague desire to win, you are really just wishing or hoping.
- It takes a team to create a winning archer.
- Enjoy the process.

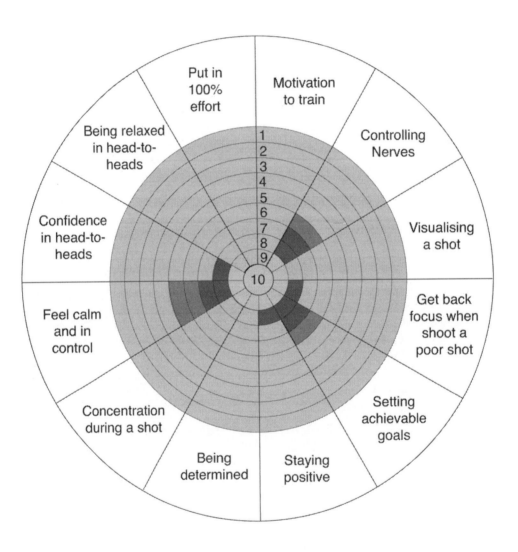

2

Assessing Where You Are

Imagine it is late at night and you are driving around but are also quite lost, so you get out your phone and call a friend: "I need directions!" you say.

Your friend asks, "Well, where are you?"

You answer, "I don't know."

"Where are you going?" he continues.

You answer, "I don't know that, either."

What do you think the odds are that you are going to get good directions? Or that your friend won't assume you are drunk or playing a prank and hang up on you? It is impossible to come up with directions when you don't know where you are or where you are going. Likewise, it is really difficult to make a plan to become a winning archer if you don't know where you stand archery-wise and where it is you want to end up. So, let's look at how you go about assessing where you are currently (at least with regard to your archery) but first let's figure out where you are going.

What is the Goal?

The obvious goal of a winning archer is to win archery tournaments, but which ones? Not too many archers win a state or national championship on their first try, so that might be a bit too ambitious. It is almost an oxymoron that learning to win consistently requires you to, well, win some tournaments. Therefore, it only makes sense to "start small" and "work your way up" by trying to win some smaller contests before you enter the bigger ones. Maybe you are a member of an archery club and there is a club championship. Or a local archery shop sponsors an indoor competition every winter. These are often quite good places to start shaping what are called your outcome goals. An outcome goal is an end in itself, not a means to an end. So, a goal of winning a tournament or placing in the top ten in a tournament or a achieving a score of such and such or making a national team, and so forth, are outcome goals. They are not ways of doing things, there are things to be done. The other goals that will become useful to you (if they are not already) are called process goals. A process goal is the means to an end. So, if your outcome goal is to win your local JOAD (Junior Olympic Archery Development) club championship, a process goal that may get you there is "I will follow my shot sequence for every shot." A process goal doesn't win you anything, but if you meet that goal, it may just get you a good enough score to accomplish your outcome goal. Basically outcome goals are used to *demonstrate* progress in archery while process goals are used to *accomplish* progress. What we are looking for now is an outcome goal.

So, the first task is to figure out what it will take to win your local tournament. Being blessed with the Internet, we can usually look up last year's winning score for almost any tournament (or better, the winning score for the last three years). If it is not available, ask around the club, archery shop, etc. Once you have that information, you can compare that number with what your average score is. Let's say, for simplicity, that the round being shot is a 300 point indoor round and that the last three winning scores for your competitive category are: 286, 279, and 281. Now, if your average score for that round is 264, you are about twenty points away from the average winning score of the last three years (283). So, you are not yet in a position to win this tournament. If your average score were 291, you would be in an excellent position to win, but it is not.

To keep it simple, if your average score equals the winning score, you have about a 50:50 chance of shooting a winning score. It doesn't mean you are going to win, but you can, at least, reasonably expect to be "in the hunt."

So, clearly you need to improve to meet this first outcome goal.

The next question is: improve what? Now we come to the "assessing where you are archery-wise" part.

What is Strong? What is Weak?

The next task in your assessment has two parts: a self-assessment and an outside assessment. What are being assessed in both cases are your form and your execution. The very best way to do this is with the help of a coach. If there is no coach available in your area, an experienced shooting partner may be able to help or you may find a coach who will give you an assessment via video clips you submit to them. Basically, you need to take a critical look at your own archery form and execution. Here is one way I do it. (You may want to use this method "as is" or modify it. I suggest you type up a form which you can then print out and also make any modifications you wish. Make the form so that "Form" or "Exection" can be selected. Include things like "Date" and "Name of Evaluator" along with any notes that may be made.)

Self Assessment–Form The physical aspects of form to assess are: stance and posture, positions of hands, full draw geometry, and followthrough geometry. Note: All of these are addressed with regard to a shot that is fairly level as body geometries are modified substantially to shoot up and down hills, for example.

Stance and Posture Is the stance open, closed, or square and to what degree? Is the torso vertical? Is the head position directly atop the spine (Your head can be tilted chin up or chin down slightly, but not to either side.) Are the shoulders low to begin with and the back relatively flat? Are the ankles, knees, hips, and shoulders in line and, if not, in what orientation are they? Are the knees relaxed and not "locked out?"

Positions of Hands At full draw is the bow positioned on the pad of the thumb of the bow hand? Are the bow hand fingers curled and relaxed? Are the knuckles of the bow hand at about a 45° degree angle to the ground? Is the bow wrist relaxed? Is the release/draw hand relaxed? (The muscles used to curl the fingers are in the upper part of the forearm, not in the hand.) Is the release hand at a comfortable angle to the ground? Are the back of the release hand and wrist flat?

Full Draw Geometry (From a Shooting Line Viewpoint) Is there a straight line from the center of pressure on the grip to the arrow nock to the tip of the draw elbow (this is called "the primary force line")? Is the torso still vertical? Is the draw elbow crease roughly vertical? Are the shoulders still low? Is the head poised over the top of the spine and not tilted? (From the Rear—Opposite the Target) Is the draw elbow in line with the arrow (compound)? Is the draw elbow in line with the arrow or, better, slightly past that line (recurve/longbow)? Is the archer leaning forward or rearward or to the front or back? Is the head tilted to either side? Are the archer's shoulders parallel to the arrow (compound) or pointed at the bow (recurve/longbow)?

There are a great many other things that can be assessed but these are the key points that need to be addressed first (*see illustration next pages*).

Outside Assessment—Form The exact same questions need to be answered by an outside observer with no communication about the observations until the process is done. This restriction is important. If you prompt your observer by saying "I think my bow shoulder is a little high, don't you think?" you may be biasing the observation you really want. If your bow shoulder is indeed high, an expert observer will notice it. If it is not, then they won't. Why cloud the issue ahead of time? Don't talk with your observer about the observations until you are both done.

Now, if this cannot be done by direct observation, you can video yourself and send the videos to your observer. It is probably best to video three shots from a face-to-face "shooting line" position and three shots from the rear (opposite the target). You should use a tripod so the angle of shooting doesn't change or move. Step off the line between shots so that your observer can see your whole shot sequence. You may want to include a "let down" in your clips. From these video clips all of the above observations can be made fairly easily and the execution items (see below) should also be visible. If you send a video of just one shot, there is no guarantee that that shot is typical, nor is there any way for the observer to tell if you are being consistent. Even with three shot clips, this is not easy. A full assessment might take hours of observation, but we are just getting started here.

Self Assessment—Execution It is really hard to "see" yourself execute shots, but since archery is a kinesthetic sport (there is a focus on the "feel" of shooting), how shots feel to you needs to be included. That said, you can also take videos and observe them yourself to see what you look like from an outside viewpoint. You can also talk to the camera about the feel of a shot as you shoot ("That felt good." or "I plucked that one.").

The Lines

Line of Sight—Once set cannot be moved

Plumb Line—
Archers need
to stand straight

Primary Force Line—
Elbow can be higher
but not lower

Arrow Line—Must
be in plane with
target center

Hip Line—Should
either line up with
heels and shoulders
or be mid-way

Heel Line—
Can be used
instead of toe line

Toe Line—
Can be misleading
if feet flared

# of Archery

Plumb Line—Archers head must be straight up and down

Shoulder Line— Parallel to Arrow Line for Compound, points to Center of Pressure on Grip for Recurve

Scapula Line

Spine Line— Should be flat and plumb

The physical aspects of execution to assess are: use of a shot sequence/routine, consistency of routine, especially consistency of release and consistency of followthrough, also the rhythm of the shot: is the draw strong and smooth? Is the time spent at full draw (indeed, all of the steps) appropriate?

Use of Shot Sequence/Routine Do you follow the exact same steps in every shot? Do you do each step the exact same way each time? If there is a mis-step at any point, do you execute a "letdown" and a complete start over? Are the steps crisply executed or are they lackadaisical?

Consistency of Release Does your release hand move just backward a short distance upon release? Does it move backward consistently (same distance, angle, etc.)?

Followthrough Geometry Is the full draw body posture held (as much as it is possible) for 1-2 seconds after release?

Consistency of Followthrough Does the bow react toward the target along the stabilizer line before moving up/down or sideways? (This is typically only an inch (2-3 cm) or so.) Is the full draw body geometry largely intact 1-2 seconds after release? Is the followthrough consistent from shot to shot?

Rhythm—Consistent and Appropriate Some people shoot quickly and others more slowly, whatever the tempo of the shots it needs to be the same from shot to shot. Signs of rushing or holding too long are noticeable. Is breath control evident? If after holding too long the archer is breathing heavily to recover, it is not.

Outside Assessment—Execution Just as with the form observations, the exact same questions need to be answered by an outside observer with no communication about the observations until the process is done. This can be done by video, but is probably done more effectively in person.

Making The Assessments

Along with any notes that you or your observer might take while making the observations an assessment as to the quality of the form or execution element on a five point scale is made. The scale is entirely arbitrary; you can make up another one if you like, or assign an A-F "grade" like in school, you just need to be consistent in its use. Some use a method of ten point scale assessments and then these are mapped out onto a FITA target. This system gives you an instant graphical idea of what your assessment is indicating (*see this chapter's facing page*). Feel free to be creative.

The five point scale goes like this:

beginner level   1   2   3   4   5   *world class*

So, if you think your full draw geometry is better than what a beginner can do, but nowhere near world class, you might rate it as a 2 or a 3. These are value judgments, so they are not assumed to be really accurate, but they should be fairly close to what you are doing.

All of these assessments have to be done before the two of you sit down to talk about them. The last task for each of you is to make two lists from the observations and assessments:

List 1–Your three best form/execution elements.

List 2–Your three worst form/execution elements.

Now, you are done.

Discussing the Two Assessments

And now you get to find out whether *your* perceptions are valid or not. Here is where having a high quality coach can pay huge dividends. There is a reason that Tiger Woods and Phil Mickelson still have golf coaches. A good archery coach, like a good golf coach, has a trained eye that will see a great deal that ordinary archers will not.

How do you know you have a good coach? I will address this question in Chapter 9.

So, you go over the two forms and share what you both observed. Realize that your coach/observer can't know what you were feeling and you can't know what he/she saw. Pay close attention to things you thought might be problems, e.g. "I think my bow shoulder is a little high." If your observer didn't notice it, maybe it is not a problem or not a big enough problem right now to require your attention. What coaches "see" are things that stand out. Our eyes are drawn automatically to those things. Possibly when some other things are addressed and made better, a "slightly high bow shoulder" may stand out enough to get noticed. Also pay close attention to where you both agree. Those observations/assessments are probably quite solid.

Last, look at the list of your perceived strengths and weaknesses. We often delude ourselves as to what our strengths and weaknesses really are. If the two of you agree to a fair amount, this is reassuring in that it tells you that your self assessments are fairly accurate. If you disagree a great deal or completely disagree, I make the following recommendation: in general, when you are a beginning competitor or just starting learning how to win, you should pay a great deal of attention to your coach's recommendations. As you get closer and closer to being an elite archer, you need to pay more and more attention to your own recommendations. This has a proviso, though: you need to be able to see yourself, in some form, from the outside. A talented coach's view is probably best, but video can be a viable substitute.

What If My Coach Doesn't Want to Do This?

Assuming you have explained the process in enough detail that your coach does understand what is involved, well, this is not the only way to do this.

What does your coach want to do?

If what they suggest sounds reasonable, try it his/her way. What you want to get is two uncontaminated sets of observations and assessments of your form and execution that the two of you will be able to discuss but you want them in writing. There is far too much information to keep in your head or for your coach to keep in his. Using a form helps because then you will at least have both made the same observations and assessments.

Having it in writing is very important because this is not the only assessment you will ever do! You will do this process fairly often to evaluate your progress. When you were lost and needed directions, most people will give you directions like "turn left at the gas station" or "if you get to a railroad crossing, you've gone too far." Every path has signposts that tell you whether you are going in the right direction. Form and execution changes that don't make scores better aren't improvements, they are just changes. You must be able to tell whether or not you have actually made a change and whether it has had any effect. Having assessments in writing enables you to look back at what you were doing "before" and compare them with what you are doing now, that is "after" the changes.

If your coach doesn't want to put his/her assessment in writing, it could be a sign that you need to look for another coach. (Here "writing" means some kind of physical record: this could be a vocal recording, he/she could allow someone to make notes that are read back to them, etc.) And the next time you do this you may have a different coach, so having the observations of the previous coach may be very helpful.

Now What Do I Do?

Now, you have the task of making changes, which you will learn how to do in the remaining chapters. Later, you will feel the need to know the answer to "Where am I now (archery-wise)?" and you will do another assessment.

While the details will be covered in those chapters, the overriding principle is the quality of all shot elements should be about the same. What use is a world class stance if your full draw posture is beginner level? The first step is always to bring all of the shot elements, form and execution, to the same level. Then the strategy is the bring all of those up to another level, a higher one, but one in which all of them are about the same level of quality. How many times you are willing to go though the work of bringing your form and execution "to a whole new level" as the sports cliché goes, will determine how high you will rise.

Assessment Plan B

Here is another form of assessment which is less formal.

Shooting a practice round is a test of performance. This is not practice per se; this is a test to see how well practice is going. Shooting practice rounds bi-weekly, or more frequently if you are practicing daily, is absolutely essential, but if this is all you do, what you are really doing is drilling your non-winning form. If you know the weak points in your form and execution, you must devise workouts that focus on bringing up those weak points until they are as strong as the rest of your shot. If you don't know what they are, you need help from a shooting partner or coach to help you identify them.

When you shoot practice rounds I strongly recommend that you must use a fresh target face for each practice round, on the back write down the date, time, location, your mental state, your physical state (tired from a long day at work/school, etc.), and any other information that may affect your performance—all written down before you begin. Now, take the target from your last practice round. Examine the patterns in the arrow holes. Are your misses more high than low . . . more left than right? If the misses are consistent and uniform, a sight adjustment might be necessary. If you are getting just occasional "flyers," form/execution break-downs are happening. Let's say your flyers are all at 6 o'clock (low); this could mean you are dropping your bow arm. When you are next practicing, schedule some time shooting in which you increase focus on having a strong bow arm and see if these 6 o'clock flyers disappear. If so, you now know what you need to work on. If the bow arm is not the culprit, maybe hand pressure on the bow's grip is varying. Check it out.

If the target face is a multi-spot face, are the patterns for each spot consistent? If you change the order in which you shoot the spots, do the patterns shift with the order? Do the groups swell on your last target due to fatigue? If you are shooting compound unlimited/freestyle, the pattern your scope dot or ring makes can provide information about these misses. Only a very accomplished shooting partner or coach can help you with these things.

This is vitally important: if you are getting bad advice or just guessing as to your problems, you will be wasting time and effort working on the wrong things! I can't say this strongly enough. Getting the very best advice you can is absolutely critical to making progress.

Acting on a Plan

Once you have gotten the analysis of what it is you need to work on, you need to create a practice plan to make positive changes and eliminate these weaknesses in your shot. (We talk about planning in detail in Chapter 8.) Why would you be working on anything but those things keeping you back? This absolutely requires you to keep written records. If you are working hard on something and you have no sign that anything is improving, either you are working on the wrong thing, or working on it the wrong way, or something else is getting worse as the thing you are working on is getting better.

There are some who believe that you should never dwell on your weaknesses, that you should only dwell on your strengths. If you are one of these folks, you have to plan your practices differently. There must be a focus on your strengths in the expectation that your weaknesses will be brought along. In any case, you need to have some measure of whether or not you are making progress.

Signs you are getting better are: smaller groups, more consistent groups, higher practice round scores, higher competitive round scores. If these are getting worse, so are you! There is a lot of evidence that says if you don't measure it, it isn't real. If you are a compound unlimited/freestyle archer working on indoor rounds, you need to keep track of X count and "inside out" X counts as well as scores of your practice rounds. The Koreans log their arrow scores as to how close to the center they were. An arrow just out side of the 10-ring, might receive a score of 9.9, for example (*see illustration right*). There are many ways to record what you are doing.

You Must Keep Records of These Things You also need to know what your range of normal group sizes are. For long distance shooting on a FITA target, you can use the scoring rings ("holding the red" means your groups are no larger than the 7-ring. "Holding the gold" means you shoot almost all 9's and 10's. For closer in shooting you may have to measure

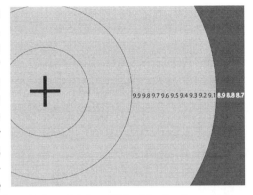

the actual group sizes (as the diameter of a circle which will hold all of your normally shot arrows). On a good day your groups will be smaller, tighter. On an off day they will be larger and looser. If you don't know the normal range of the sizes of your groups at competitive distances, how will you know whether or not what you are doing is at all effective?

If one drill doesn't seem to be working, maybe another will. Some people are being limited by their equipment, this must be examined if you are shooting flyers. It is not unusual for a top archer to go back to a previous bow/arrow setup to test themselves. Can they still shoot the kinds of scores they shot (or even better scores) with their older rig? If better scores can be had, then you know you have improved (because that old rig hasn't changed). And if the older rig can produce better scores than your new rig, maybe you need to look into your new rig's setup and tune. It is not uncommon to need help in doing this.

If your records are complete, you might be able to identify equipment problems better. If you put new cables and a new string on your compound bow a couple of weeks ago and your scores have softened from what they were before that change, I would double check all measurements and settings on them. If you changed arrow rests, put the old one back on and check to see whether your groups are better, etc. In order for you to win, your equipment, form, and execution must all be "on."

Written practice plans, keeping records of changes in your equipment and practice scores are key elements in your success; don't give this advantage away.

Practice Scores v. Competition Scores A really important piece of information is how your practice scores compare to your competition scores. There are two common patterns. One type of archer thrives on competition. This archer is energized and focused by an event. Her scores at competitions are higher than her practice scores. The other type of archer tenses up and generally performs worse in competition than she does in practice. The question is: what does this information tell you?

First, if your competition scores tend to be 3-4% higher than practice scores, then your practice scores only need to be close to the level of a winning score for you to be ready to compete and win. If your practice scores are higher than your competition scores, you must set your practice score goals even higher to account for that. There are implications for the way you practice also.

Sidebar: A Note for Coaches

Obviously, if your student is eleven years old, you must modify this process. You can do your part as the outside observer, but the archer is probably not yet aware of many of the things that are important to observe. One way to bridge this "maturity gap" is to take photos (video or still) of your archer from the two positions recommended on several different shots and ask the more straightforward questions from the form: "Are you standing straight? "Are your shoulders 'low'?" "Are you holding your form after release?"

It is important to engage young archers in this process in some form as it helps to develop the relationship between the two of you as well as helping the young archer to understand what he/she is being asked to do.

Any modification of this process that improves athlete-coach communication should be considered worth doing. In general, I would spend less time on this process the younger and more inexperienced an archer is and more time, the more experienced (regardless of age).

Key Points
Chapter 2 Assessing Where You Are

You can't tell where you are going if you don't know where you are and you certainly can't tell how fast you are getting there! Assessment is critical to winning.

- It is really difficult to make a plan to become a winning archer if you don't know where you stand archery-wise and where it is you want to end up
- An outcome goal is an end in itself, not a means to an end. A process goal is a means to an end. Basically outcome goals are used to demonstrate progress in archery while process goals are used to accomplish progress.
- Assessments have two parts: a self-assessment and an outside assessment.
- Assessments are of both form and execution.
- An assessment made by video and sent to a distant observer is viable, but some care must be made in taking the videos (using a tripod, consistent shooting angles, etc.) and in shaping the assessment.
- You need to be able to see yourself, in some form, from the outside.
- When you are a beginning competitor or just starting learning how to win, you should pay a great deal of attention to your coach's recommendations.
- As you get closer and closer to being an elite archer, you need to pay more and more attention to your own recommendations.
- Assessments need to be in writing; no one's memory is good enough to keep track of all of the details over years of time.
- Form and execution changes that don't make scores better aren't improvements, they are just changes.

- The quality of all form and execution elements needs to be about the same. The first step in getting better is always to bring all of the shot elements, both in form and execution, to the same level.
- How many times you are willing to go though the work of bringing your form and execution "to a whole new level" as the sports cliché goes, will determine how high you will rise.
- If shooting practice rounds is all you do, what you are really doing is drilling your non-winning form.
- If you are getting bad advice or just guessing as to your problems, you will be wasting time and effort working on the wrong things!
- Getting the very best advice you can is absolutely critical to making progress.
- If you are working hard on something and you have no sign that anything is improving, either you are working on the wrong thing, or working on it the wrong way, or something else is getting worse as the thing you are working on is getting better.
- Signs you are getting better are: smaller groups, more consistent groups, higher practice round scores, higher competitive round scores. If these are getting worse, so are you!
- If you don't measure it, it isn't real. If you don't write it down, you will forget it or mis-remember it.

Steve Ruis

3

Winning Equipment

Introduction

In John Holden's 1987 book *Shooting Straight: A Guide to Archery Equipment* he describes a survey he administered to British archers over a three year period that showed unequivocally that "At least 75 per cent of target archers and hunters are struggling under a severe technical handicap." By "technical" he did not mean shooting technique but "equipment." In another claim, he stated "In at least 75 percent of cases, there was no indisputable relationship between an archer's shooting *expertise* and his *results*" (his italics, not mine). He went on to claim that "Over 90 per cent of beginners give up within three years of first drawing a bow. . . ." It has been a long time since Mr. Holden did his research but I expect that if it were to be repeated, the results would be similar, if not worse.

Exacerbating this is the fact that in the U.S. there is a declining number of archery shops which have people on staff who are target archery specialists. Which leads directly to the question: how are you supposed to get good equipment and get it into shooting shape?

A simple answer would be to buy the best available equipment and then you wouldn't need to worry. The problem with this approach is that top end equipment is often temperamental (the archery term is "critical") which requires an elite archer's skill to master. Until you have that skill, buying the best of everything can actually impede your progress as an archer. This chapter explains how to evaluate your own equipment and shows you how to make sure it is set up correctly.

How Good Does My Equipment Need to Be?

If you read Chapter 1 or the introduction above you know that I don't think you need top of the line equipment to be a winning archer. There is a prevailing tendency to believe otherwise because, well, in part it is the American way! Contributing to this impression are the marketing practices of the major archery manufacturers. One of their prime marketing tools is sponsored archers. These folks get reduced prices on, or free, bows and arrows, money, etc. for the companies' right to brag when they win a tournament. (It is actually more complicated than that, but that is the gist of the arrangement.) The advertisements show a photo of Winner Y with a big check and a marketing pitch about how much their bow (or arrows or fletches or bowstring . . .) was key in that win. This happens in many sports, not just archery (consider golf or skiing, as examples). In some years it was the case that a single bow manufacturer swept an entire year's competitions! (It was also the case that anyone with even an outside chance of winning had been sponsored by that company.)

Now, I am not trying to blame the manufacturers for this situation, they aren't doing anything different from NASCAR. (C'mon, do you think those cars have anything to do with the Chevy or Ford you can buy at your local dealership?) But, you can't afford to buy into a misconception. To make the point, just pick a favorite professional or elite amateur archer of yours. I would guess that three years ago they were winning tournaments. Two years ago, same thing. Last year, they won, right? More than likely they shot a different bow each year because the manufacturers tend to come out with new models every year. And, all of the top sponsored archers have to shoot the most recent bow in the line because the manufacturers stop selling last year's bow and the bow of two years ago, so advertising it doesn't make them any money. (In fact, winning with last year's bow would send the wrong message, a message that you do not need this year's bow to win!) So, for the last three years, this archer has won but: it was with different bows. So, which do you think is the more important part of that combination: the bow or the archer? Uh, huh, it is the archer. Everyone understands that this is the case . . . well, everyone except those of us who wish to delude ourselves that there is some magic in a new bow.

I am here to tell you that there *is* magic in a new bow, but it is not what you think. A new bow gives you increased focus and some enthusiasm. It sends you back to the basics of bow setup and bow tuning. I think new bows are cool for these reasons and more. But I understand that the bow, itself, will not add many points to any of my scores because of its better design or better materials. It might actually improve my score a little, but that is probably due to the bow being fit to me and my style of shooting a little better than the previous bow. Archery engineer Bob Ragsdale has insisted for years that all a bow does is provide an arrow with it's initial velocity. It does nothing else. We hope they do this consistently and, by and large, they do.

Let's look at what you really need from your equipment to enable you to win and win consistently.

What Should I Want from My Equipment?

This is a better question. Knowing the answer to this question will enable you to determine whether or not your equipment is up to the tasks you set it.

The key phrase from John Holden's book was that an "indisputable relationship between an archer's shooting expertise and his results" has to be created. You want your good shots to be good because you shot them that way and you want your bad shots to be bad because you messed up. Yes, you want your bad shots to be bad! If an arrow aimed at the three-ring lands in the center, unless there was one heck of a wind blowing one has to wonder whether one aimed in the center will land in the three-ring later. What you are looking for is equipment that gives you good feedback on your shooting technique.

During practice and competition, shots go wrong from time to time. When these things happen, the first thing the archer needs to determine is "What is the source of that bad shot?" There are three sources of the problem:

1. environmental conditions (wind, rain, etc.)
2. your equipment (none is perfectly reliable)
3. you

If you are trying to adjust your equipment for a problem of execution or blaming an equipment problem on the wind, you are in deep, deep trouble. You will be trying to fix the wrong problem.

I had a young friend who I coached a bit from time to time, and who was at my house shooting 50m in the back yard, ask me "Why would my groups all of a sudden get really tall?" We walked down to the target and sure enough, his group was about ten times as tall as it was wide. I started into a discussion of all of the things he could be doing wrong and he eliminated them one by one as he pulled his arrows and we walked back to the shooting line. As he drew his next arrow, the right half of his launcher rest blade cracked and fell off of his bow. "That could be it, too," was my comment.

Basically, all a bow does is impart the initial thrust to your arrows. The arrows, once they receive that thrust, fly through the air according to the laws of physics. But, boy can we make things more complicated than that!

What we want from our equipment is simple: we want it to be reliable, consistent, and durable.

A set of aluminum arrows all of which have been repeatedly bent and then straightened will be none of the above. Such arrows will bend easier, have spines which are considerably different from when they were first purchased, and will break more easily. Arrows don't last very long, but bows do. Three years ago I saw a guy shooting in the Compound Unlimited shoot off at the WAF Vegas Shoot, the biggest indoor money shoot of the year, with a bow that was ten years old at the time. That bow may have been an older model, but I would guess that his strings and cables were well short of two years old and that critical parts of sights and arrow rests were refurbished or replaced recently.

Whatever the source or age of your equipment, in order for there to be an "indisputable relationship between an archer's shooting expertise and his results," your equipment must be properly fitted to you and properly set up, tuned, and maintained.

Getting the Right Gear

You may already have the right equipment for you. Or maybe you don't. How can you tell? The critical point here is, if you purchased the wrong gear, either it will be very expensive and time consuming to "make it right" or it will be impossible to do so. You may want to replace it. But whatever you do, your decisions must be based on what works for you.

Let's take the critical equipment piece by piece (we will ignore for the time being things like armguards and quivers).

Compound Bows

The critical fitting factors for compound bows are the draw weight range, the draw length, and the physical mass of the bow.

Compound Bows—Draw Weight Being able to adjust the draw weight (draw force) over a wide range is one of the most useful aspects of compound bows. When it comes to choosing arrows, if you want an arrow that is a bit on the stiff side, you can decrease the draw weight a few pounds to dial it in. If you want to use an arrow that is on the weaker side of the range of possibilities, you can raise the draw weight a bit to tune it in. So, it is nice to have some draw weight available on either side of where you are shooting a bow.

There is some talk that always circulates about "wanting to shoot a compound bow at the top of its draw weight range" or the bottom of the range or . . . or. . . . Generally this is misinformation based on good information. Typically a compound bow will be most efficient near the top of it's draw weight range (with a heavy arrow) but the differences in efficiency inside the entire range of draw weights are small and really have no effect on the bow's ability to be reliable, consistent, or durable. But somebody read an article about this fact and translated that into "shooting a compound bow at the top of its draw weight range is *better*" which is an oversimplification and incorrect. Archery's oral tradition is full of erroneous advice such as this. A compound bow can be shot well at any draw weight within its given range. Where you want to be cautious is trying to shoot such a bow *outside* of that range of draw weights. Below the bottom of the range, the bow may become "spongy" or seem very loose and will become unreliable. Above the range (and yes, there are things you can do to increase the draw weight beyond the factory settings but I am not going to describe them here as they are potentially dangerous), you get a similar loss of reliability (and durability). Actually, I try to be somewhat away from either the top or bottom of the range specified. This gives me some room to adjust the bow's draw weight for tuning purposes.

A compound bow is a somewhat complicated machine and is best shot within the specifications set by the manufacturer.

The draw weight that is best for you is probably not what you think. There is, more than likely, quite a wide range of draw weights that you can handle. Most people would be better off closer to the bottom of that range than to the top. The reason for this is lightweight carbon arrows. Arrows? Yes, light, stiff carbon arrows fly faster than the arrows of the past. Even if you shoot long distances or unmarked yardage shoots, both of which convey an advantage to those with higher arrow speeds, you do not have to shoot the highest draw weight you can manage to get those arrow speeds anymore. Lower draw weights, along with creating less fatigue, allow for more relaxation at full draw and that, more than anything else, is critical to better aiming and execution of the finish of your shot. The best advice I have to offer you is to experiment and to ignore most of the "common wisdom" that is available on Internet talk sites. There are good reasons to want to shoot more draw weight, but if you think you have one, be sure you set up tests to see if actual improvements to your scores occur when you try them.

Compound Bows—Draw Length Bows of just a few years ago had limited draw length adjustments. Today's bows often have a great deal of draw length adjustment built in to them. There are some technical arguments about the advantages and disadvantages of compound bow eccentrics (cams, etc.) that can be adjusted over a large range. Without getting into those, again it is best that you stay well within the range of adjustments indicated by the manufacturer's specifications.

Also, you may need to adjust your draw length to within 1 mm/⅟₁₆″ as this measurement is critical to being steady while aiming. The problem with incorrect draw lengths is that compensations are made in your form for incorrect draw length settings. Most noticeably draw length and stance affect one another, as do draw length and full draw body posture, so if you change one, you affect the others.

Being at your correct draw length is so critical that professional archers will spend hours adjusting the draw length of a new bow until it is just right, down to an adjustment of a half twist of a cable. Some will shoot groups at longer distances and then make changes of a single twist of a cable and shoot again to see whether the groups get better or not! Of course, these guys have gotten the draw length set very close to where they know it should be before they start such a procedure.

Having a good coach or a very experienced archer help you with this task can save you a lot of time. The marker to "rough in" your draw length is the view from behind when you are at full draw. You can set up a camera on a tripod and try to do this alone, but having a trained pair of eyes is much better. What you are looking for is whether your draw elbow is aligned with the arrow (when there is a likewise straight line (as seen from face on to the archer) from the center of pressure on the grip to the arrow nock to the tip of the draw elbow (*see photos on p. 14-15*). If your draw elbow is swung around toward your back past that line, your draw length is too long. If it is outside of that line, it is too short.

Realize that if your bow arm is not coming straight out from your bow shoulder this test will be wrong. You must have correct upper body geometry for this to work.

Compound Bows–Physical Mass I see a great many archers with bows that are too heavy for them. A heavy bow is a stable bow, so you will see a great many pros who have actually added extra mass, in the form of back weights and side weights, to their bows. Archers trying to emulate these professional archers do likewise and end up with a bow that is too heavy. What this leads to is form flaws such as "dropping your bow arm." Mostly these archers are deluding themselves into thinking they are in control because they use their draw arms to help them lift the bow.

Then, when the draw arm becomes disconnected (at release) the bow immediately begins dropping. You should be able to lift your bow into position easily and comfortably with no help from your other side. To test whether a bow is too heavy, pick the bow up and hold it in full draw position (without using your draw arm) and count to ten (one thousand one, one thousand two, etc.). If you can do this you are minimally strong enough. If you can manage a count of 20, without grimacing or overtly straining, you are definitely okay. If you can't manage a count of ten without dropping your arm or making adjustments to your posture, you need to remove any extra mass until you have developed your bow side deltoid muscles (the upper arm muscles used to raise your arm) until they are up to the task. You can compensate for a little extra mass by widening your stance a bit. For a lot of extra mass, all you will get trying to shoot such a bow is bad habits that you will have to work hard to correct later. (Digging yourself out of a hole you dug yourself is a terrible waste of effort.)

Recurve Bows
The critical fitting factors for recurve bows are the draw weight at your draw length, your draw length, and the physical mass of the bow.

Recurve Bows–Draw Weight Since the advent of the three piece takedown recurve bow (the three pieces are: the top limb, the riser/handle, and the bottom limb) things are much more easily adjusted than before. Where compound bows have large draw weight adjustment ranges, recurve bows do not. The draw weight of any particular recurve bow can be adjusted by no more than about 10%, so for a forty pound bow, about four pounds of adjustment is possible (compared to a similar compound bow which would have ten or more pounds of adjustment). If you need a bigger adjustment than that, you need new limbs.

Typically, recurve archers start at lower draw weights and as their technique and physical conditioning improve they move to higher draw weights. Sometimes younger archers struggle with "making distance," often when they move into an older age grouping and their competitive distances increase. But with the advent of lightweight carbon arrows, this is much less of a problem than it was in the past. So, why is higher draw weight desirable?

At any given draw length and with a standard arrow, if you increase the draw weight/draw force, you will increase arrow speed. A faster arrow is more stable (a little anyway) but more importantly it spends less time in the air to be affected by wind or rain. It also means that your bow arm at full draw will be closer to level for most distances.

But draw weight, like other factors, is susceptible to what I call the Goldilocks Principle. Too much is not good. Too little is not good. What we are looking for is "just right." If you have too much draw weight, you will not have good enough technique to control it; having too much draw weight requires you to use extra muscle which will lead to fatigue and making mistakes. If you have too little draw weight, you will need to elevate your bow too much to make longer shots, making full draw geometry harder to replicate and there is less tension on the bowstring at full draw making small mistakes in the release more detrimental to your score.

The correct amount of draw weight is "just right" and here is a test to determine whether yours is "just right" or not. This test was developed by Coach Kim, H.T. of Korea:

Draw your bow to anchor, hold for seven seconds comfortably, then let down to predraw position for two seconds. If you can do this eight times in succession without strain, your draw weight is correct. If you can only do this 3-4 times, it will be difficult to learn to shoot well. If you can do this ten times, your draw weight can be increased.

Recurve Bows–Draw Length The draw length of recurve bows and longbows is not set as an adjustment of the bow as it is with compound bows, but the bow must be long enough to allow for the correct draw length. Generally slightly taller bows, are easier to shoot than shorter bows which tend to "stack" (increase in draw weight per inch goes up at higher rate) near the end of longer draws. Many of the Korean female archers are looking at shooting 68″ bows even though they would be shooting 64″ or 66″ bows based only on their heights. The longer bows sacrifice a little arrow speed but are smoother to draw, hence reduce the amount of archer fatigue during long shooting days and during tense shootoffs.

If a clicker is used, the clicker needs to be set so the draw elbow is inline with the arrow line when seen from the rear or, better, the draw elbow is slightly past the arrow line. The draw weight needs to be measured at this position as a measure of the "weight in hand." This is the "draw weight" value used in all of the arrow spine charts.

Recurve Bows–Physical Mass In general recurve bows are lighter than compound bows, but it is possible to have too much mass in hand. Typically this is a problem for youths and people with little upper body development.

To test whether a bow is too heavy, pick the bow up (with all of your accessories attached) and hold it in full draw position (without using your draw arm) and count to ten (one thousand one, one thousand two, etc.). If you can do this you are minimally strong enough. If you can manage a count of 20, without grimacing or overtly straining, you are definitely okay. If you can't manage a count of ten without dropping your arm or making adjustments to your posture, you need to lower the weight of the bow or use a lighter bow until you have developed your deltoid (upper arm) muscles. You may also want to add strength to your deltoids through weight training.

Arrows

This is the one area where spending your money wisely pays the biggest dividends. It is also where the most tuning takes place. The most critical fitting factors for arrows are spine and shaft length.

Arrow Spine Arrow spine is a measure of an arrow shaft's resilience, its ability to resist a sideways force (some say it is a measure of shaft stiffness). Compound/

Sidebar—About Growing Archers

If you are a young archer and haven't achieved your full growth, there are additional considerations. Basically, did your mom ever buy shoes for you with "room to grow?" You need to do the same for your archery equipment. The limiting factors are it must be useable now and it must be able to be adjusted to be useable later. For example, when buying a compound bow for a younger archer, I want to get a draw weight range, e.g. 45-60 pounds, so that your current draw weight is at the bottom of the bow's range of draw weights. In this manner, as you grow and get stronger, the bow can be adjusted to a greater draw weight. If your current draw weight is 42 pounds and you buy a 30-45# bow, you are basically going to have to buy a new bow to move up much in draw weight. But if you get a 45-60# bow, you will have a lot of room to move up in draw weight. This doesn't mean you can't go out and buy another bow, it just means you aren't forced to by needing to increase your draw weight, a common adjustment made by growing archers.

Similarly, if you know you are going to be growing taller, you don't want a bow to be at the high end of any adjustment it has for draw length. You would rather be near the low end. (Draw length increases with height.)

For recurve archers, it is more complicated. First, there are quite a few different manufacturers, then there are, commonly, 23″, 25″, and now 27″ risers available (among others) and short, medium, and long limbs (typically available in 2# draw weight increments). In general, if you expect to grow in height a great deal, try to get the longest riser you can physically handle. This will allow you to have a bow that is "long enough" for quite some time and you can make draw weight changes by buying new limbs (longer limbs accommodate a longer draw length).

Riser and Limb Combinations of Three-Piece Recurve Bows

A Riser Length of	with Short Limbs makes a	with Medium Limbs makes a	with Long Limbs makes a
23″	64″ bow	66″ bow	68″ bow
25″	66″ bow	68″ bow	70″ bow
27″	68″ bow	70″ bow	72″ bow

Because young people don't develop the deltoid muscles on the tops of their upper arms (used to raise their arms) until quite late, you must be leery of trying to shoot a bow that is too heavy. Most all compound bows are near to being too heavy for young people and changing to a metal-risered recurve from lighter wood- or plastic-risered recurves creates this situation, too. You can compensate to some extent by widening your stance a bit, and you can train those muscles (the deltoids) to be stronger, but you can pick up bad habits while these adjustments are being made.

To test whether the bow is too heavy, pick up your bow, take your stance, and raise the bow (bow hand only) into full draw position and count to ten (one thousand one, one thousand two, etc.). If you can do this you are minimally strong enough. If you can manage a count of 20, without grimacing or overtly straining, you are okay.

release archers can choose from a fairly wide range of shaft spines whereas recurve archers are much more limited in their choices. There is no more critical factor regarding arrows than to have a spine match to your bow/technique. The reason I include your technique as a determinant of the needed arrow spine is the spine we are talking about is called the *dynamic spine*, which is based on the behavior of the arrow as it is shot. The spines listed in arrow charts are what are called *static spines*, which are measured on a spine tester while the arrow is not moving. In fact, static spines are measured on the shafts alone, before fletches, nocks, and points are added. So, manufacturer spine charts can be used to get an arrow shaft that is close to your requirements, but you must determine how to set up those shafts (by adding fletches, points, nocks, etc., and by cutting them to the length you want). Here is a procedure for doing just that.

Compound Arrow Setup We start with compound arrow setup because it is the simpler of the two. Typically, you pick a shaft from the manufacturer's spine chart based on the shaft you choose. For shooting long distances outdoors people tend to use 1¾" to 2¼" vanes but you can choose almost anything you want. Ideally you would want the least amount of vane area you can shoot consistently. You can choose whatever nock you want, also. For point weight, most field archers shoot 8-9% FOC (front of center) and most target archers are in the 13-14% FOC range. The shafts you must buy uncut. Once you have the components ready, you are ready to assemble them. Attach vanes to all but two of the shafts (if you want to do bare shaft testing, which I recommend) and nocks to all. Insert points into three of the fletched and the two unfletched shafts. Now you do a bare shaft test, starting at 10-15 yd/m.

The bare shaft test (*see sidebar*) is quite sensitive if you shoot with your fingers on the string. It is less sensitive if you shoot with a release aid, but it still works for this purpose. The bare shafts should be impacting at about the same height as the fletched shafts at this distance. If they are not, adjust your nocking point height until they are. Now, assuming your centershot is acceptable, the bare shafts will impact to the left of the fletched shafts if they are too stiff and to the right if they are too weak (switch left and right here if you are left-handed). Your initial test should show the shafts as being too weak as you ordered them uncut and spine charts are set up for arrows cut to your draw length, that is they are adjusted for arrow length. What you don't want to do under any circumstances is to directly cut the arrows to your draw length! If they are even ½" too short, you will be going back to the shop for another set of shafts! Arrows that are too long can be fixed; arrows that are too short usually can't be fixed.

After you have confirmed that the arrows test weak, remove the points, cut ½" off of the five testing shafts (Only!) and reinsert the points. Then you retest. This is tedious but it has the advantage of only messing up five shafts of a dozen if you make a mistake and, once you get an excellent set up (as shown by the bare shaft test—see below), you have a recipe for all of the arrows you will shoot out of that bow for as long as you use it. You simply keep testing and cutting until the bare shafts group with fletched arrows. You may want to cut just ¼" at a time when the bare shafts start getting "close" to the fletched shafts. When you are satisfied with the bare shaft test, you cut the other shafts to that length and insert points in those.

Some people want to confirm the correct shaft length by stretching out the bare shaft test to 20, even 30 yds/m. The farther the target, the farther the bare shafts will hit from the fletched, so the test becomes more sensitive at longer distances, but do not start at a longer distance, because a badly out-of-tune bare shaft can fly almost sideways and get broken when it hits.

Also, a great many very good shooters like to have the bare shafts land slightly below and slightly to the left (to the right if you are left-handed) of the fletched shafts. This is because they prefer a slightly high nocking point (giving them a little extra clearance between vanes and arrow rest thus causing the bare shafts to land a little low) and a slightly stiff arrow (which they consider more forgiving of slight launch errors and which causes the bare shafts to land a little to the left). You may or may not have this preference, but there is a great deal you can read in the literature of archery about tuning your arrows. See the references at the end of this chapter for some of these.

You should then "group test" these arrows. In every 1000 shafts, points, fletches, etc. there are pieces that do not match the specifications correctly. You could start by weighing all of the components and spine testing all of the shafts and checking the straightness of all of the shafts before you begin (some folks do) or you could just test the final product. Any arrows that don't group with the rest need to be set aside and checked to see what is wrong with them. If you can't figure out what is wrong, set them aside for blank bale shooting only.

When I am being especially careful, I will weigh all of the fletched shafts to see that they all weigh the same (within 1-2 grains) and weigh all of the points, too. I can then match the heavier points with the lighter shafts to get a set of arrows that are more evenly weight matched. If I am being a bit lazy, I will make up two dozen arrows and weigh each of them. From those I will pick out two sets of six arrows that are weight matched very, very well, and probably have another six I will just use for practice.

There are lots of ways to do this. There have been quite a number of articles in *Archery Focus* magazine about just this topic. Heck, the Internet is almost full from discussions on this very topic!

The big advantage compound archers have is you can fine tune the spine match of your arrows to your bow with draw weight adjustments. If the arrows are just a bit too weak, take one quarter or one half turn off of both limbs and retest. A test that says "arrows too weak" is equivalent to "bow too strong" for those arrows. Similarly, if your arrows test a tad too strong, you can add draw weight in half or quarter turn increments to "dial them in." If you have to change the draw weight several pounds, the arrows were not close enough to be dialed in. A compound bow's draw weight and draw length are the critical values in bow setup and shouldn't be changed significantly to get a set of arrows tuned. Tune the arrows to the bow (and the archer), not vice-versa.

Recurve Arrow Setup This procedure is different from the compound procedure only in a couple of fine points: one is the clicker, if one is used, another involves the finger release and arrow rest side pressure.

Ideally a clicker's arm is roughly perpendicular to the arrow, which means that the attachment point of the clicker needs to be just above where the arrow point will be at full draw. If your clicker is attached directly to the riser, you want your arrow point to be roughly even with the front of the bow. Consequently you may have to manipulate arrow point mass to allow for this length (keeping a reasonable FOC balance, etc.). If the arrow protrudes more than an inch (2-3 cm) or so from the bow, you may want to consider a clicker attachment that allows the clicker to hang from your sight's extension bar.

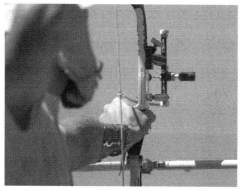

The other point is that many recurve archers want the arrow to rest such that the "front node" of the arrow is on, or is just behind, the pressure button contact of the arrow rests. The reason for this is when a bowstring is loosed using a finger release, even the cleanest finger release does not allow the string to push into the arrow directly down the shaft of the arrow. Instead, the string slides off of the fingers/tab so that the rear end of the arrow is traveling forward and sideways simultaneously. The first reaction of the arrow is to buckle, but because it is a stiff, resilient column, it bends back . . . and forth . . . back . . . and forth as it flies toward the target (50-60 vibrations per second). These oscillations are mostly side-to-side and continue for a considerable distance from the bow.

The nodes, slightly in from each end, move very little (side-to-side) as the arrow travels down its path (see figure).

node   node

line of flight

Whether you are using a finger release with a recurve bow or a compound bow, the effect is the same, although compound bows tend to show less buckling because initially there is less force being exerted by the string on the arrow (due to letoff) and if a release aid is used, which provides a much smoother release the string, the amplitude of the oscillations is typically smaller and they tend to be more up and down than side to side. Arrows are not shot perfectly from any bow because of compromises we make in nocking point locations (to keep the shaft on the rest) and centershot locations (to compensate for bow hand torque, etc.).

Finally we get to the role arrow nodes play in making a shot. The effect of arrow nodes occurs in the first centimeters or so of travel of the arrow. Here are three scenarios:

Arrow Node at Cushion Plunger In this scenario, at full draw the arrow's front node sits at the cushion plunger button. The string is loosed, the arrow bends such that the middle of the shaft bends into (toward) the bow. The short section in front of the node bends away from the bow. Since the node, which does not move sideways, is at the button, the button neither absorbs nor provides any force. As the arrow slides forward, the shaft starts to bend back as it slides along the rest, but the button acts freely without out any preload.

Arrow Node Behind of the Button If the arrow node is behind the button, the sideways flex of the shaft pulls the shaft away from the button, which provides no cushion effect.

Arrow Node Ahead the Button If the arrow node is ahead of the button, the segment just behind the node slams into the button, compressing it too much, causing the button to shove the shaft too far out from the bow.

All of these scenarios (save the first) are heavily affected by the quality of the loose of the string. Of course, having the front node on the button (or ever so slightly behind) creates the setup least affected by the quality of the loose from shot to shot. The "ever so slightly behind" is part of the recommendation because the arrow starts sliding on the rest even as it is bending, so there is a short amount of time while the first bend is forming for the arrow node to get up to the button.

Before you get all gung ho in setting your arrows up this way, consider the most important aspect of making any such changes—before you consider making any change in your bow-arrow system, you need to ask if this change is going to have a positive effect on your archery . . . and, if so, how much?

My impression is you have to be a very, very good archer before this is worth doing, that is the effect is small. It is way more important to improve your form (if you have weaknesses), get a good arrow spine match for your setup (if that is lacking), and many other things. On the other hand, I like to do everything I can to make my equipment as forgiving as I can (which I often do with my outdoor setup over the winter and my indoor setup over the summer).

Of course, your arrows have to be fully made up, because changing point weight, fletching, etc. will affect the position of the nodes in the shaft. The procedure to find the front node is fairly simple. You need a rigid fulcrum, like the lip of a baking dish or the edge of the trough of an Arizona *Arrow Straightener*. The arrow is held horizontally by its nock, gently but firmly, and rested on the lip of the baking dish near the point (*see photo*). Firmly pluck the arrow downward near the middle of the shaft with your other hand. The pluck sets the shaft to vibrating (slightly). If the arrow is resting at the arrow node, there will be very little movement of the arrow and very little sound. If the arrow is resting ahead of or behind the node, the vibrating shaft will skitter around on the lip making sound. The rest is trial and error (move the contact point up and down the shaft until there is no sound/vibration). When you find the node, mark its position with a marking pen and repeat the process with 2-3 other arrows. They should all have their nodes in the same place (roughly, as this is a crude test). Also, it is more complicated that I am portraying it here: for example, the front nodal point of the arrow when on the string is somewhat farther back than the front nodal point of the arrow in flight (because the rear of the arrow is still attached to the string). But don't worry about the complexities as they are probably too small to have much effect.

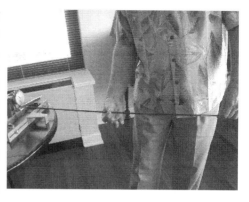

Expect to find the front node quite close to the front of the arrow, 3-5 in being common, but because there are so many arrow sizes, and point sizes, and shaft materials, you will just have to find it on your own.

Whatever you do, do not change your draw length to get the arrow node in position! The distance from the node to the front of the shaft is the amount of arrow overhang (past the button) you will build in when you cut your next batch of arrows. If this is a significantly different overhang than you have had, you will need to retune your bow-arrow setup (because you have changed the shaft length).

If you want to figure this out before you build your arrows, you can just slip in a point to an arrow shaft and test it that way. It should get you close.

Tuning

Any further adjustments you make are a form of tuning and the final arbiter of such changes is group testing (see sidebar). No whiz bang tuning scheme can replace group testing as the ultimate goal is to have all of your arrows in the highest scoring ring on the target, which requires that your average group size be somewhat smaller than the size of that scoring ring. If your groups are bigger than that ring, you will not be able to get all of your arrows into it except by luck and winning archers don't count on luck. Not that luck doesn't exist! I scored an X on a 35 yard target when my thumb brushed my chin and triggered my release before I had gotten to anchor. (This is one of the reasons I no longer use a release aid with a light trigger.) But luck is not a basis upon which you can build consistent scoring.

If you make a change and your groups get smaller, that is a good change! If not, then not. Period.

God is in the Details

The heading for this section is a quote from a famous architect. It has since be morphed into "the Devil is in the details" but however you take it, the details are important when it comes to your equipment. Since archery is primarily an individual sport, it is probably best that you be the only one responsible for your equipment, which means you need to be aware of the details. Since I didn't want this book to be a 1000 pages long, I left out a few topics in this chapter, things like: bow sight setup, nock fit, arrow rest setup and tuning, high-speed video analysis of equipment, eccentric timing, string and cable maintenance, D-Loop tying and tuning (Yes, you can tune your D-Loop), release aid setup and maintenance, tab setup and maintenance, waterproofing of your equipment, storage and handling of your equipment, testing arrows for cracks and other defects, spin testing arrows for concentricity of points and nocks, . . . , need I go on?

I have supplied an extensive list of recommended sources for further information at the end of this chapter as there is so much to learn. (The book "Simple Maintenance for Archery" by Alan Anderson and Ruth Rowe is an invaluable place to start your learning of "bow mechanics" unless you have an archery tutor who will patiently teach you everything you need to know.)

Summary

It is key that once you get your equipment and you set it up so you can get an "indisputable relationship between your shooting expertise and your results" you need to measure up everything and record those measurements in your performance journal. The lengths of all strings and cables, the final draw weight, brace height, tiller measurements, the length (and manufacturer) of your fletches, point weight, arrow FOC, everything! . . . because you must be able to maintain this system. If you replace the bowstring on your recurve bow and you use the same length of string with the same number of strands, but use a different string material, you may have to retune the setup. Having written all of that stuff down means you have a chance of replicating your setup. (See Tom Dorigatti's brilliant articles on this very topic for more detail. These (as well as all back issues) are available at www.archeryfocus.com with a subscription.)

Winning archers are always looking to learn if there is anything new to learn, be they 18 or 80 years old. Even if you delegate something like string making, for example, to someone else, you still need to know how to check a string for wear, to tell if it is faulty, and to tell if the serving and your nocks fit adequately, plus more. Some archers won't shoot strings made by other people because if they lose a tournament because of an equipment failure, they don't want to be blaming somebody else for that failure.

The wisest thing I heard anybody say about archery equipment is a guy who remembered his baseball glove as a youth and how it was lovingly fit, broken in, and then used until it became an extension of his hand; it felt like a part of him. That's what he wanted from his bows and arrows.

I agree.

Sidebar—Bare Shaft Testing

A "bare" shaft is simply an arrow with no fletching on it. When I build up a set of arrows, I typically put nocks and points in the whole dozen but I fletch only 10, leaving me with two "bare" shafts.

Here's how bare shaft testing goes. Start reasonably close in to a target, 10 yards/meters being a good starting point, although you can expand the starting distance to as much as 30 yd/m. (But don't start there, if something is really out of whack, you can break an arrow or bare shaft doing this.)

The test is simple: shoot three regular arrows and two bare shafts. If the three fletched arrows do not make a nice group, start over. If the two bare shafts don't group, you shot them differently—start over. If you don't feel you shot all five arrows the same way—start over. After five quality shots, the thing to look for is where the two bare shafts are compared to the fletched shafts. If they are high or low as in this graphic, you must adjust the nocking point locator to correct for this (move the nocking point locator down if the bare shafts are low and vice-versa)

If the bare shaft group impacts to the left or right of the target (see graphic), you adjust the centershot (the left-right position of the arrow rest). If the bare shafts group to the left, move the arrow rest to the right, and vice-versa).

Sometimes, no amount of arrow rest change does the trick, or the arrow rest is so far out of normal position that something else has to be wrong. If this is the case, the spine of your arrows is questionable. This is a case of poor set up as getting a bow and arrows to fit you is what set up is all about. But, occasional tweaking of the arrow's spine is necessary. For a right-handed archer, if the bare shafts impact to the left of the fletched arrows, the arrow is said to be "too stiff" or "over-spined." If the bare shafts impact to the right, the arrows are said to be "too weak," or "under-spined." If your student is left-handed archer, you have to reverse all of the left-rights! Here are some ways you can go about it.

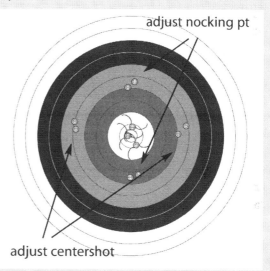

adjust nocking pt

adjust centershot

Here are some options to correct a "too stiff" or "over-spined" arrow.

• increase draw weight of the bow

- add point weight
  And if you have a recurve bow . . .
- decrease the side pressure on the arrow rest (button pressure)
- increase brace height

  Here are some options to correct a "too weak," or "under-spined" arrow.
- reduce draw weight of the bow
- shorten the shaft (a little at a time)
- reduce point weight
  And if you have a recurve bow . . .
- decrease brace height
- increase the side pressure on the arrow rest (button pressure)

Of course you can get combinations of some of these. The general procedure is to handle nocking point location first, then centershot, then arrow spine.

Sidebar—Group Testing

This method is easy to describe, but arduous to do. Group testing/tuning is the Cadillac (I said Rolls Royce before but I didn't want to leave out domestic manufacturers.) of all tuning methods as it tests what we really want to do—shoot high scoring groups of arrows.

Here's the procedure: shoot groups of 5-6 arrows at different distances. You can take pictures of the groups with your cell phone or keep a clipboard with a target drawn on it and mark the locations of all of the arrow impacts. The shapes of the groups should be round and the sizes proportional to the distance, that is the group at a distance two times as far should be 2X larger (2X taller, 2X wider), if 3X farther it should be 3X larger (3X taller, 3X wider). Here's a figure to show what I mean (see right).

The group at 40 yd/m is twice the size of the one at 20 yd/m. The group at 60 yd/m is three times as wide and tall as the one at 20 yd/m. The groups are all roughly round. The group sizes are proportional to the distances shot.

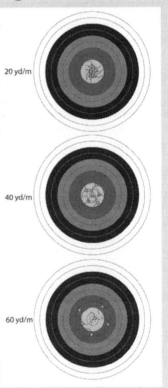

20 yd/m

40 yd/m

60 yd/m

Now, here's the hard part with regard to tuning. The above is your baseline. You then make small changes (in nocking point height, centershot, and rest side pressure—one at a time). And then you test for grouping, after each change generally at a longer distance (long for whatever style of competition, division, etc.). When you get a better group (defined to be still round, but smaller), you test the other distances. (The reason for testing the other distances is you can make changes that make shooting a particular distance better but other distances worse.)

Then you make another change and retest.

This can take a very long time! So, this is considered something only advanced archers do. Group sizes are a gauge of how well you are shooting. If your groups are getting smaller, you are becoming a better archer. If your groups are getting larger, you are getting worse. Realize that every time you make a big change, it can take three weeks of practice to make that change be comfortable, and for that time your group sizes will suffer. Only after that change has been fully adopted can you determine whether the impact on your groups sizes has been positive or not. The tuning changes in the tuning procedure are very small ones ($\frac{1}{32}$″ in nocking point height, for example) so the impact of that change shows up immediately.

And, everybody has good days and bad days, so you need to know what your group sizes are on good and bad days. (The better you become the less differences there are in your groups sizes on good and bad days, though.) The group sizes (and the consistency of those sizes) shot by other archers give you an indication of how good they are.

This is why group testing is the Cadillac of all tuning tests.

Also, see the article "Group Tuning: A New Approach" in *Archery Focus* magazine for some ways to make group tuning less arduous.

Further Reading
Books and Videos

📖 *Handbook of Modern Recurve Tuning—Start to Finish* by Richard Cockrell
While a little rough around the edges, you would be hard pressed to find a more comprehensive guide to tuning recurve bows.

📖 *Bow and Arrow*, by Larry Wise—Great book from a master coach, archer, and bow mechanic on all aspects of compound bow equipment (available from Stackpole Books, 800.READ-NOW).

⊙ *Bringing Arrow Building Home* (presented by John Kleman)
This video "how to" covers building and maintaining arrows (available from The Bohning Company, 616.229.4247).

⊙ *1 Cam vs. 2 Cam Bows—Beyond Tuning*, by Larry Wise

Master archer and coach Larry Wise compares the differences between round wheel and cam bows, one and two cam bows and even shows how to plot a draw-force curve (available from *www.robinhoodvideos.com*).

🕮 *Mastering Bow Tuning* by James Park
Australian James Park has written a number of books like this one which came out first as eBooks for easy distribution.

⊙ *Professional String Making* (presented by Larry Wise)
This video covers everything you need to know about building strings, cables, yokes, tied-on nock locators, D-loops, etc. (available from *www.robin-hood-videos.com*).

🕮 *Simple Maintenance for Archery* by Ruth Rowe and Alan Henderson
Every archery instructor needs a copy of this book! Step-by-step procedures for building arrows, tying on nocking point locators, replacing center servings, etc. (available from www.qproductsarchery.com).

⊙ *Understanding Arrow Flight* (presented by Bob, Terry, and Michelle Ragsdale) If you prefer a video approach, this video from the Precision Shooting Equipment (PSE) Corporation describes all of the steps in building arrows.

🕮 *Tuning Your Compound Bow, 4th Edition* by Larry Wise
Great little book from a master coach and archer (available from Target Communications, *www.deerinfo.com*).

Articles from Archery Focus Magazine

This may seem a little self-serving, but I hope not. *Archery Focus* magazine (yes, I am its Editor) is an OnLine subscription-based magazine which provides six new issues per year but also provides access to all of the articles it has ever published! You get all of the back-issues for free.

The OnLine Edition was designed as an archer's and coach's repository by its creators and we are continuing with that. Subscribe for a year and then you can read, download, and/or print any of hundreds of articles (over 1000 at last count, not counting editorials, etc.). The whole idea is to get the information out to people who can use it. More information, including sample articles, is available at *www.archeryfocus.com*.

Key Points
Chapter 3 Winning Equipment

Equipment selection, setup, care, and maintenance is tricky. Some archers are good at it, others aren't. Everyone needs help with their equipment from time to time.

- Until you have the skill required, buying the best of everything can actually impede your progress as an archer!
- What you are looking for is equipment that gives you good feedback on your shooting technique. You want your good shots to be good because you shot them that way and you want your bad shots to be bad because you messed up. (A sign you are improving is the quality of your misses improves!)

- We want our equipment to be reliable, consistent, and durable.
- In order for there to be an "indisputable relationship between an archer's shooting expertise and his results," your equipment must be properly fitted to you and properly set up, tuned, and maintained.
- Whatever you do, your decisions must be based on what works for you.
- There is, more than likely, quite a wide range of draw weights that you can handle. Most people would be better off closer to the bottom of that range than to the top.
- Draw length and stance affect one another, as do draw length and full draw body posture, so if you change one, you affect the others.
- A heavy bow is a stable bow. A bow that is too heavy is a disaster.
- Young people don't develop the deltoid muscles on the tops of their upper arms (used to raise their arms) until quite late, you must be leery of trying to shoot a bow that is too heavy.
- Most tuning is done with the arrows, not the bow.
- There is no more critical factor regarding arrows than to have a spine match to your bow/technique.
- Once an arrow shaft spine is selected, the correct length can be found by bare shaft testing a small set of them and slowly reducing the length of those shafts and retesting until the length is perfect.
- The final arbiter of equipment changes is group testing.
- It is key that: once you get your equipment and you set it up so you can get an "indisputable relationship between your shooting expertise and your results," you need to record everything you can think of about that equipment and setup in your performance journal.

This was considered championship form in 1987: floating anchor, mouth open, low draw elbow, tense draw hand included. None of these characteristics is considered good today.

4

Winning Technique

How Good Does My Technique Need to Be?

Many people believe that winning archers must have perfect form and perfect execution to be consistent winners. Uh, no. Here's the truth of it, with regard to shooting an arrow: "You don't have to do it right, you just have to do it over." (Bernie Pellerite) As mentioned in Chapter 1, the 2008 men's Olympic gold medalist had two aspects to his shooting that most coaches would regard as "form flaws" and recommend that they be corrected. Your technique doesn't have to be perfect but it does have to be yours. This means it has to suit you; it has to suit your physique and it has to suit your temperament. In general, most people's form is very much the same; the differences are small. But those small differences are critical. What you want is form and execution that is optimal for you.

I don't mean to harp, but a good coach can pay large dividends when it comes to adapting standard form to you and finding your optimum form.

Standard Form

Most technical books on archery, which includes the vast majority of target archery books, typically focus on what the author considers to be "standard form," essentially what those authors considered to be optimal form (see photo at left, optimal means "best or most favorable"). For example, if you are shooting a recurve bow and you try various draw lengths you will find one of those draw lengths gives you the smallest group sizes (the typical indicator of better performance). If your draw length is shorter than the optimal value, your groups get bigger. If your draw length is longer than the optimal value, your groups get bigger, also. This is nothing new. It applies to draw weight and all of the other aspects of bow setup and form (how open or closed your stance is, how much muscle is used to stand still while shooting, everything).

To the extent that your form differs from what is optimal for you, your ability to score well will suffer. It is that simple. But, what many of these books don't tell you is that it is very hard to quantify how much it will suffer from any suboptimal form element. For example, the above mentioned Olympic gold medalist, Viktor Ruban, puts the thumb of his draw hand behind his neck. Very, very few coaches recommend this practice because it can lead to quite a few bad habits and there is no particular advantage to doing so. And, there is always a cost in using a suboptimal technique element. The cost is typically additional training time that wouldn't be needed otherwise or additional energy being expended while shooting, which leads to fatigue and mistakes made from fatigue. Was the cost high enough, in this case, to lose an attempt to win an Olympic gold medal? Apparently not. The point here is if you could put a point value on "doing it differently" or "being suboptimal" and that point value was, say, two points in a 120 point Olympic Round match, could that two points be offset by something else, for example a feeling of confidence and comfort in shooting your shot your way? In many cases, it most likely is. I am not advocating that you invent new ways to shoot arrows from a bow or that you insist on doing it "your way." What I am advocating is that standard form is quite probably near optimal for the vast majority of archers and will only be modified slightly to make it near optimal for you. But, I am also saying that you shouldn't spend large amounts of time and effort on minutia as the very tiny aspects of your form and execution probably will not make the difference between winning and not winning. An archer who trusts his form and is confident in it is way ahead of someone who isn't, so once you have your form in good shape, the best path is usually to practice it until you are very confident in your ability.

Finding Your Optimal Form

This is not a technique book, by design, but an example is needed here to demonstrate how one goes about finding one's form. The example I give you is finding your optimal stance. Actually stance is too big of a topic, I am going to limit the example to foot positions.

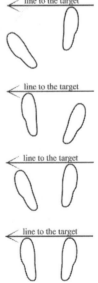

Stances and Foot Positions You already have a stance. You most likely know that your feet can be open, closed or square to the target (see diagram). Which of these should you use? Clearly, any stance from which you can't swing the arrow so that it points at the target won't work. But there are a great many stances left to choose from.

In the absence of outside forces (other than gravity), the most stable arrangement is to have your hips in line with your feet and your shoulders in line with your hips. The argument is that any twisting between feet, hips, and shoulders requires muscles to be involved and muscles get tired and therefore function differently over time. Lining up feet, hips, and shoulders is a "neutral" body position that doesn't require that extra muscles be incorporated to maintain that. (Some archers deliberately twist their torsos and use that muscle tension to make their bodies more stable, especially in the wind, etc. but that practice is another discussion.)

This means that with the arrow pointing at the target, a compound archer's feet should be in a square (or "parallel") configuration because the shoulders are parallel to the arrow, and so should be the hips, and the feet parallel to the shooting line with a line across the shoe tips being perpendicular to the shooting line and parallel to the arrow.

This means that with the arrow pointing at the target, a recurve archer's feet should be in a slightly closed configuration because the shoulders are about 10-12 degrees closed to the arrow, so then should be the hips, and the feet parallel to each other but a line across the shoe tips should be pointing about 10-12° to the right (for a right-handed archer) of a line to the target.

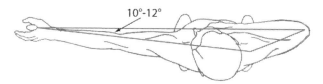

So, why does almost nobody shoot this way? (Most archers shoot with open stances.)

First of all, it would be a mistake to assume that any archer has been instructed by a trained coach or that they have read any of the technique books. And don't assume the technique books make any kind of consistent recommendation regarding foot positions, either.

What I recommend to all of my student-archers is that they start with a square stance. A square stance is relatively easy to adopt, easy to repeat, and *it is near optimal*. And then I recommend that they don't change it unless they can prove there is a better one for them.

I don't want to rant, but the vast majority of archers will "try" a new form element and, after a relatively short trial, if they "like it" they will continue using it. Worse, they will see some pro winning doing something and incorporate that "thing" into their form in the hope that it will produce better results. Then they will make a change from that change based upon a buddy's recommendation. This is not a recipe for success, far from it. Any change that doesn't produce better scoring is not worth your time and effort. Changes that are not improvements can mislead you into thinking that you are making "improvements" all of the time when, in effect, you haven't gotten any better and there is an excellent chance you have gotten worse! And, if you go about things this way and stumble upon perfect technique for you, you are going to change it yet again and it will no longer be perfect for you. Don't delude yourself; always test whether any change you make is an improvement or just "a change."

First let's look at some methods for finding "your stance," at least the foot position part of it.

Finding Your Natural Stance One method, which I found very attractive when I first heard of it, was a technique to find your natural stance. The point was that your body has a natural tendency built in regarding where to point the bow. If you position your body other than in your natural stance, you will have to incorporate some muscle to swing the bow onto the target (and muscle gets tired, etc.). The procedure goes like this: take your stance and bring your bow up and center your sight on the target, draw and anchor and "settle in," then close your eyes. Count to eight (one thousand one, . . .) then open your eyes. If your sight aperture isn't pointed exactly at the center of the target (in the left-right sense, not up-down) move your feet until it is. You repeat this process until you can draw on the target, close your eyes, count to eight (slowly) and then when you opened them, the arrow is pointed in the right direction. This stance is your natural stance. You then have to practice with this stance until it became "normal," that is habitual for you. A problem with this procedure is that the rest of your form elements have to be quite good to find your optimal natural stance. If your draw length is too short, you will come up with a different stance that if it is too long or just right. So, if you want to use this procedure, you will probably want to repeat the drill several times as your technique becomes refined.

A Stance Identification Drill Coach Larry Wise, one of the finest compound coaches in the world, came up with a beautiful drill to find your optimal stance. In Larry's technique you take two three dot (40 cm) target strips and mount them sideways and end-to-end. You then take a square stance aligned to the center of that strip and shoot arrows at these targets at 18 meters/20 yards without moving your feet. (This can be more or less distance, but not by much.) You must shoot in a nonsequential order—you can shoot all of the targets from left to right one time then next from right to left, then in random sequences, etc. but you can't keep shooting in just one sequence. If you shoot them always from left to right, for example, and your fourth shot is technically weak (due to shot timing, breathing, fatigue, etc.), you will get poor performance on the fourth target every time for reasons that are unrelated to stance.

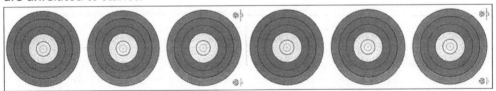

Shoot these targets for a number of days or weeks and then look at the patterns made. The three targets to the left represent three degrees of closed stance; the three targets on the right represent three degrees of open stance. If one of the targets shows clearly superior grouping, the stance associated with that target is your best stance. If the leftmost or rightmost target shows best grouping you will want to repeat the experiment aligning your square stance with the left edge (if the rightmost target proved superior) or right edge (if the leftmost target proved superior). This will give you six degrees of open stances or closed stances, respectively, to compare. Again, you are looking for the target with the best grouping of arrow holes to identify your best stance.

Another Stance Identification Drill *Archery Focus* author and compound coach Tom Dorigatti came up with a novel way to tune one's stance. He has you shoot at an indoor target with your eyes closed. It goes like this: put up an NFAA five spot target and draw on the first spot and settle on the first spot, when you have done so, close your eyes and finish the shot. Repeat for the other four spots. If your stance isn't correct for the other elements in your shot, you will consistently see your shots off to the right or left of center. If the arrows were to the right, it is because once your eyes were closed and you had no way to correct for any body drift, your body turned to the right. To correct for this, move your feet to the left and retest.

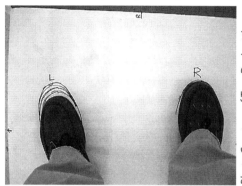

Photo Courtesy of Tom Dorigatti

Because this can be exacting and arduous, Tom recommends you stand on a large sheet of cardboard (4´ x 4´). He draws on a shooting line, then when you take your first stance, he draws an outline of your shoes with a marking pen. After you make each stance adjustment, he makes a new outline in a different color of ink. When you have found your optimum stance, you can use the cardboard to make sure your stance is correct as you practice it until it becomes habitual.

The Elements of Technique Training

The drills/exercises described above can help you find something close to your optimal foot position. The next question is: How can I make this mine? How can I *own* this new form element? In answering this question, I will answer it in general while using the stance/foot position example, because all such training is done the same way.

One Thing at a Time, Please When you are competing, the one thing you don't want to think about is how to make a shot. This is known as being self-conscious, that is being aware of yourself doing something. This is what makes teenagers gawky and makes new learners clumsy. Do you remember learning to drive? Do you remember learning to tie your shoes? Have you ever watched a three- or four-year old trying to learn to tie their shoes? It is painful to watch. It is slow, arduous and rife with mistakes.

Have you ever met an adult who had to think about tying their shoes? No? Neither have I. But, it is important that you realize that repetitive tasks, like tying your shoes or driving a car, do not become automatic. You can still make mistakes. And you need to know what to do when you do make a mistake. What do you do when you flub tying one of your shoes? Do you go back to "first, hold the strings out straight, then lay the left one on top of the right . . . "? Of course not, you merely "focus" on the task a bit more than before and *voila*, the shoe is tied. If you make a small mistake while driving, you drive with a slightly heightened awareness for a bit, then relax back into your normal mode of driving. But this "focus" is quite nebulous, no instructions or guidance is forthcoming to help with the task.

"Just who, then, is tying your shoes and driving the car, if not 'you?'" you ask.

This capability is called your subconscious mind.

"Does your subconscious mind just know how to do these things?"

No, you have to train it.

"How do you train it?"

You train it consciously. Your subconscious mind is attracted to what is important to you, what you focus your attention on, and by how much intensity you bring to any task. Take a look at that three-year old learning shoelace tying. Talk about being focused; there is nothing in that child's mind but that task. This is how we learn to do such things.

So, the lesson is:

1. You must focus on just one thing you want to learn at a time.

2. You must be intense in your training, and

3. You must be emotionally involved.

You probably understand Points 1 & 2 easily, but what about the third point? What emotions are involved? What this means is you want to be emotionally engaged with what you are learning. When things go right, you want to feel good about it-not ecstatic good, just pleased. When things go wrong, you want to adopt a stern corrective stance, a little like a piano teacher who says: "No, that is not right, do it again correctly." But, you do not want to get angry with yourself when you make repeated mistakes! Strong emotion will imprint the situation on your subconscious mind (which is why we tend to remember traumatic events for very long times) and make an image that your subconscious mind will interpret as "something important" to you which will make that mistake easier to repeat in the future. The emotions needed are calm expressions of pleasure and disapproval.

If you leave out the focus, don't bring the intensity, and are emotionally uninvolved, you may still learn the task, but it will take much longer or you will learn the lesson much less well.

Practice, Practice, Practice Once you know what to practice, you then need to practice it. To practice a new stance, you could put down your cardboard template and just take a stance over and over. I would find doing this boring and this approach (sheer repetition) is not the most efficient way to learn something. A better way is to place your template on the shooting line, take your stance and execute a good shot. Then step off of the line and repeat. In "normal" shooting sessions, you step onto the shooting line, shoot a number of arrows (without moving your feet) before stepping off. By stepping off after every shot, you are increasing the repetitions of "taking your stance" by quite a bit. In addition, you are practicing in context, in the context of shooting a shot. In addition, you must bring the necessary focus, intensity, and emotion while taking your stance.

Or you could do this but every second shot includes drawing with your eyes shut and opening them once you have settled in at full draw. Imagine how reassuring things would be if you find yourself pretty much on target shooting with your eyes closed! This has to reinforce the "rightness" of your stance.

Now, most importantly, the last point:

4. You must not evaluate any shot on any basis but upon the element you are practicing.

So, after every shot with your new stance, you might look down to see if your feet were correctly in the outline on the cardboard. If so, "Yes!" If, not . . . "No, that isn't right, do it over correctly." Whether the shot hit the target center or the wall is not pertinent at this time. It is a truism that if you expend a great deal of focus on one part of your shot, the other parts will degrade. So, you must always train with this knowledge. The focus required on a new element will temporary make you a poorer archer. When the "new" becomes "normal," then your focus will be redistributed evenly and your shot will come back, hopefully to a higher level.

If you want, after a while of doing this you can take a couple of shots at a different spot on the line and see if you can recognize what your new stance looks like without the cardboard. Then go back to the cardboard. Try taking your stance without looking and see how close to being correct it is by comparing it to the outline on the cardboard. These are just different ways to get you to focus on your new form element and the variety helps break up the monotony of repetition.

In the future, you will always take your stance and then check to make sure it "looks right" and "feels right" each and every time you step to the line. This is a necessary habit.

Testing A Stance How does one test a stance? The procedure, again, is simple; the prime criterion for quality of shots taken is group size, so you need to shoot a number of groups at your test distance or test distances. To measure group size, if the groups are centered (and they always should be), you can use the target rings to judge the group size. If all 5-6 arrows are inside of the 8-ring on a 10 ring target, you can call that group size an 9.0. If no arrow is even half way out in the eight ring, you can call is an 8.5 group. If just one arrow is a hair outside of the 9-ring, you can call it a 8.9 group. Other devices are to use a string or tape measure to measure the perimeter of the group. This works even if the group is off center.

Then you compare before and after group sizes. If you are an accomplished archer, don't expect big changes at short distances. Make sure that you use enough distance to spread your groups out enough to get a good reading.

"When" Can Be as Important as "How"

Many archers ignore a very important question, namely: "When is the best time to make form and execution changes?" There are a couple of opposing strategies behind the common answers to this question. One answer is to do it "now." The argument is "why would you want to practice doing it wrong or differently from what you will be doing it?" The other answer is "after the outdoor season." The argument here is that the lull between outdoor and indoor competitive seasons provides some time to make changes and then the indoor season allows repetitive

Sidebar—Form from Biomechanics

The reason "standard" archery form exists at all is due to certain principles of biomechanics. Biomechanics is the application of the "mechanics" of simple objects from physics (force, energy, leverage, mass, etc.), to living things (the "bio" part). Here are a couple of examples of applying biomechanical viewpoints to archery.

The Full Draw Force Line In standard form there should be a straight line (as seen from face on to the archer) from the center of pressure on the grip to the arrow nock to the tip of the draw elbow (*see photo p. 14*). The argument goes like this: if the center of pressure–nock–tip of elbow is not a straight line, then you will have to either "kink" your wrist, or adjust your fingers on the string. In either case, your fingers will have a difficult time acting in concert (together). The string will move the way the bow is made to move it, but the draw force has to be applied so that a clean release can be made. If using a release aid and the force line is kinked, you will be pulling on the string either up or down or left or right, which will increase the variation in the path the string takes after it is loosed, which leads to larger groups.

Recurve archers strive to have their draw elbow slightly beyond the arrow line (as viewed from the rear). This is a form of "insurance." If the elbow is just in line with the arrow part of the shots will be with the elbow slightly rearward and part slightly forward of that line, due to normal variation. We are not machines, we do not have perfect full draw body geometry. But, since having one's elbow short of the arrow line can lead to plucking the string (a major mistake), it is better to have the elbow slightly behind the arrow line as its "normal" position because when the elbow is not quite to that position, it is probably no worse than being in line. This elbow position is "pluck insurance."

Bow Hand Position Beginners in archery almost always "grab" a bow using what is referred to as a "pistol grip." Their fingers wrap around the grip of the bow and then they hold on for dear life. Subconsciously, they are trying to prevent dropping the bow (it is embarrassing) and they are preparing for the muscular activity of drawing the string (having only the vague idea that it is "difficult"). Elite archers are trained out of these intuitive measures. The bow hands of elite archers have the grip centered on the pad of their thumbs. The rest of the fingers are relaxed or curled along side the bow, not around. The biomechanical reason for this is that the string is released about 15-20 thousandths of a second before the arrow leaves the bow. During that time, the only contact between archer and bow is at the bow hand. If the archer moves the bow during that time, the shot will not be as aimed. (The good news is that our reflexes are not good enough to move the bow on purpose in that time; the bad news is that we can anticipate the release and "program in" the movement. This is what happens when an archer tries to "help" an arrow into a target center. Some archers are actually quite good at this but it is not a recommended practice.)

Also if the bow hand isn't relaxed, the bow will rebound off of the hand differently for different levels of tension in the muscles in contact with it, and the levels of tension are affected by fatigue, competition pressure, and other factors. Isolating the contact of the bow onto just the pad of the thumb minimizes the number of muscles that need to be relaxed to allow the bow to recoil from the bow hand the same way shot after shot.

The reason this counterintuitive bow hand is standard form is that the bow arm is out of the force line. We shoot by standing beside the bow, not within it. Therefore, there is always a sideways force coming into the bow from the bow arm. The bow hand can either reduce or accentuate this force. By the bow being set upon the one big muscle of the pad of the thumb and that muscle being relaxed, the bow is launched off of a reasonably soft cushion each shot. This is repeatable (relaxed is relaxed, soft is soft, whereas "tense" is variable) and minimizes the force of the bow arm onto the riser.

Standard form is shaped by the basic geometries of shooting a bow and biomechanics. No one is exempt from these criteria, but everyone is slightly different, so standard form must be adapted, albeit slightly, to each archer. Significant deviations from standard form are accompanied by a cost, either in score or in additional training time to overcome the handicap this creates.

practice and competition as the rounds and distances shot vary hardly at all and many external conditions (wind, rain, sun, etc.) don't come into play indoors.

My recommendation depends on the situation of the archer. If we are at the beginning of a competitive season and it is an important season (to make a team, meet a goal, etc.) and the changes being discussed aren't large, I will usually judge that the changes can wait until between seasons. On the other hand, if the events in the season aren't that important, and the changes are substantive, I will not recommend waiting.

If you have a coach, this is a good thing to discuss with him/her when you plan to make such changes.

Key Points
Chapter 4 Winning Technique

Most "how to shoot" books are on this very topic, so the topic here is different. Instead of describing optimal form, for example, we are going to show you how to find your best form. Then once you've found it, how to drill it until it becomes habitual to you.

- To the extent that your form differs from what is optimal for you, your ability to score well will suffer.

- You do not have to have perfect form and perfect execution to be consistent winner.
- Don't change any part of your form or execution unless you can prove there is a better one for you.
- Any change that doesn't produce better scoring is not worth your time and effort.
- To train in a physical task, you must: focus on just one thing at a time, be intense in your training, and be emotionally involved. (Yes, I said emotionally!)
- When learning new techniques, practicing in context (while shooting) decreases boredom and links the new technique element to the rest of your technique more quickly.
- You must practice, not just "fling arrows."
- When practicing specific aspects of technique you must evaluate shots only on the basis of the element you are practicing. (If working on your stance while shooting, if the stance was good on a shot, that repetition was "good" no matter where the arrow landed.) This is why archers take down the target face when drilling technique; it only provides irrelevant feedback.
- If you expend a great deal of focus on one part of your shot, the other parts will degrade, and you must expend a great deal of focus on anything new you are learning, so outcomes (scores, etc.) always get worse before they get better.
- There are good and bad times to make technique changes, and they depend on your situation.

Steve Ruis

5

Winning Physical Training

Much of what you have read about physical training (warming up, stretching, building strength and power, etc.) just doesn't apply to archery. Think about football players who are trying to get ready for forceful collisions with other players, basketball players getting ready for jumping as high as they can, running fast while changing direction, and wrestling over loose balls, baseball players getting ready for running and diving to the ground to catch balls and swinging a baseball bat at balls thrown at 90+ mph near them . . . and archers? We stand and pull a bow a few times, then we sedately walk to the target and pull our arrows and walk back (or forward) to the shooting line and do it again. No high speed direction changes, no violent collisions, no huge exertions. But, hey, we have to stand out in the hot sun from time to time, for like hours!

If you think I am going to try to talk you out of physical training, you are quite wrong. What I want to talk you out of is using what you have learned about physical training so far.

But, it is probably best to start at the beginning.

Do I Need to Do Physical Training?

This is an important question. I *think* the answer is "yes." I say "I think" the answer is yes because I have been looking for years and I have yet to see anyone even attempt to *prove* that physical training is needed for winning archery, let alone anyone actually supplying the proof.

There are all kinds of "reasons" that your archery will benefit from some physical training. If you are into field archery, there are field courses laid out in quite strenuous terrain that will kick you in the nether reaches if you aren't prepared. Courses with much elevation change involve a lot of walking (climbing!) up and down hills. Sometimes even standing is difficult when the ground is very uneven. Courses at high elevation can stress your ability to extract oxygen from the air and cardiovascular fitness becomes an issue. Standing out in the hot sun, with a drying wind, can sap your energy and strength. A FITA Round with warm-ups can involve in excess of 160 arrows shot. For a 40 pound bow, that is the equivalent of almost 3.5 tons of lifting (40 pounds at a time). A FITA Round also includes several miles of walking back and forth to the target. Tournaments that put you through the wringer physically can require you to get up the next morning and do it all over again. Basically, if you are tired, you will neither focus nor function well.

On the other hand, there are indoor competitions in which you shoot in controlled heat and humidity a grand total of 30 arrows per day. And, have you looked at photos of the people on winner's stands? When you check out the adult winners, especially on the compound side, do these people look like fitness aficionados to you?

The limited amount of research literature I have found indicates that having some extra leg strength and core strength can support better performances, but the actual archery-related scientific literature is really quite skimpy. In general, I think you will be better off with some kind of physical training regimen, but the better question is not the "yes–no" one but "What kind of physical training do I need to do?"

What Kind of Physical Training Do I Need to Do?

I hope you have read the above introductory material and not just skipped to this point because the "need" part of this question is more than a little debatable. Many an archery champion has looked like they prepared for the championship with hot dog eating contests rather than with fitness routines. But, let's start somewhere; let's start with stretching.

Do I Need to Stretch? The purpose of stretching muscles is not to prevent injuries. That idea has been debunked. In fact, inappropriate stretching causes more injuries than it prevents. Stretching muscles elongates the muscles and relaxes them. The elongated muscle then has more power associated with it because it can contract over a longer distance (which creates more force and if that force is applied over the same amount of time as a shorter contract, there is more power, too). A "tense" muscle is already contracted to some extent and therefore can only contract a bit more, thus limiting power and strength.

Do archers need more power?

Uh, no.

So, why stretch?

There are certain cases in which stretching is a good idea. Consider the fact that archery posture has you looking over your bow shoulder for long periods and while under physical tension. If you don't stretch the muscles in your neck, you may find yourself trying to get into good posture by forcing a position, rather than falling into it. If you've ever finished a shooting session with a soreness in your neck, the cause may have been a lack of length in an opposing muscle group. (Skeletal muscles work as antagonistic pairs. Contracting one skeletal muscle requires the relaxation of the opposing muscle in the pair. An easy example is the biceps of the upper arm which is responsible for bending the arm and the triceps which opens the elbow joint (*see photo*). If you tense both muscles, as body builders do when they are "posing," you can't really move your arm.

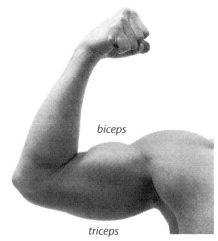

biceps

triceps

For recurve archers, stretching their neck muscles and their chest muscles allows for the rather extreme position of the head over the shoulder and for the alignment of both shoulders with the bow hand at full draw. Compound archers do not have full draw posture as extreme as do recurve archers and can often perform at high level with little to no stretching. (I do know that as I have gotten older, more stretching seems better than less.)

Realize, also, that we want to be able to stand still while under the tension of the draw. Unfortunately, few of the fitness gurus address the subject of conditioning for standing still. (As I am writing this I have commissioned a series of articles for *Archery Focus* magazine on exactly this topic. I am not a fitness expert and it is hard to get real experts to address this topic, so I am happy to have this series.)

So, stretching is . . . basically only needed to deal with physical problems that are unique to you: if you have neck muscles that lock up overnight in bed, that sort of thing, and those areas of your body that need extra range of motion (neck, chest, etc.). You don't need stretching so much as you need "warming up" and muscle activation. (There are "stretching " routines whose goal is warming up and activating muscles, so don't assume everything is cut and dried.)

Plus there is this little factor that while you are relaxing and stretching a muscle, you are actually deactivating the muscles you are stretching. If you don't activate those muscles before using them you are going to find your normal steady shot is now more than a little loose and shaky.

I also know that this "attitude" is more than a little controversial and if you encounter a "oh, you must stretch before shooting guy" please ask them to "prove it." If they seem as if they can, please send me an email (steve@archeryfocus.com) because I am going to want them to write an article about it. They will be the first in print with actual proof that stretching benefits archer's performances.

Do I Need to Activate My Muscles and Warm Up Before Shooting? Absolutely! Hey, if you talk to bowhunters they will tell you they sit still for hours in cramped little tree stands, then draw a 70 pound bow to shoot at a passing deer. And the danged deer has never done a warm-up in it's life. But, more than a few bowhunters have had extreme muscle soreness and even injuries from this procedure and, let's face it, they may only take a couple of shots a day (mostly in camp). As a target archer, it is not uncommon to take 100-150 shots in a competitive day.

So, if you are willing to accept the fact that your first several arrows shot in competition are going to be really shaky, you can forego this. But, the procedure that most people use—wave their arms around a little, use a stretch band a bit, and then shoot some arrows at targets—is far from being the "best."

Instead, a little brisk walking will help to wake up your body (that was asleep a short while ago or sluggishly sitting in your car) and get the blood flowing through your blood vessels. The "warm up" that people are talking about is getting blood from the interior of your body to the surfaces more quickly (your heart beats faster and stronger under "load") and your skin actually warms up. Then the muscles you will be using need to be put through their paces just a bit before you begin shooting at the practice butts. Some simple calisthenics suffice. The program I am recommending (below) is proprietary (means "for pay") so I am not going to describe the warm up exercises but they take only about five minutes to do and activate the legs, hip joints, arms, shoulders, and core quite nicely. The muscles get a nice little wake up and your joints get full lubricated without the full pressure of your bow being involved. Exactly what we need.

At a few field events there can be substantial waiting between targets. I carry a stretch band with me so that I can warm up after one of these breaks and not go into my next shot "cold." I likewise warm up after lunch breaks. I didn't seem to need this as much when I was younger.

Do I Need A Cardiovascular Exercise Program? Uh, need, uh . . . okay, having some kind of cardio program will help you to stay steady, keep your heart rate down when the pressure to win cranks up, that sort of thing, plus it is just plain good for you.

Many people equate cardio training with jogging. I do not. Jogging is not as useful as you would think. If you want a cardio training program look into "interval training" and things like "speed walking" or "rope jumping." The interval training will give you an effect as big as a jogging program but will not take as much time and brisk walking is available everywhere even where jogging is not. Jumping rope is something you can do at home.

But, if you like jogging, I say "go for it."

Should I Join a Gym to Have Access to Free Weights and Exercise Machines? Absolutely not. In fact, you don't need to do weight training, as it is formally constituted, at all. Now, if you like going to the gym and working out, be my guest. But it is not *necessary*. In fact, some of the things available in commercial gyms are counterproductive when it comes to archery. In general, you want to do exercises while you are supporting your own body weight. Actually your body weight is enough weight for most any program. Occasionally you might need a small free weight (<10 lb.) or a stretch band. The "weight" you need to master is "draw weight" and your bow will supply you with enough exercise with regard to that. No "archery-specific exercises" are recommended.

By supporting your own body weight while training, you are developing the "stabilizer" muscles that attend the muscles being worked. Exercise machines are designed to "isolate" muscles so they can be exercised in a concentrated fashion. But archery muscles, like the rotator cuff in the shoulder joint, are small muscles that can't move much weight and work in concert with the muscles around it (actually "them;" the rotator cuff is a cluster of small muscles). Since our desire is to stand still while shooting, we want to work out the stabilizer muscles that are responsible for stabilizing the joints and major muscle groups and you can't do that by isolating first one muscle and then another.

So, What Kind of Program Do I Need?

One program like the one you need was developed by an archer who used to be in the information technology business but left it to go back to school and become a physical trainer. His program is called the Triple X Archery Conditioning Program and is available at *http://fitforarchery.com* (The creator of the program is currently updating his program as we are going to print. *SR*) Only a few "props" are needed and you can do the entire program in the comfort of your own home. You don't need expensive gym equipment, nor do you need ongoing gym fees. And, as an archer of a few decades experience, Tim Goodwin (originally from England and now from Luxembourg) knows archery and he knows physical training. This is highly recommended.

Also, I receive no financial benefit from recommending this program. I use the program myself and paid for my copy of the materials out of my own pocket. Too many people are recommending things they are getting paid to recommend.

And there are other goodies available at the "Fit for Archery" web site, such as a nutrition program, but I haven't checked any of these out in detail. If you do and find them helpful, drop me a note. Also, it looks like he is giving away the warm-up routine mentioned above as a marketing freebie.

Note: For specific recommendations on what to do to "warm up" at the practice butts, see Chapter 10: Competing to Win.

Key Points
Chapter 5 Winning Physical Training

Much of what you have read (or can read) about physical training (warming up, stretching, building strength and power, etc.) just doesn't apply to archery.

- I "think" physical training helps archers.
- Stretching is basically only needed to deal with physical problems that are unique to you and for those areas of your body that need extra range of motion (neck, chest, etc.).
- You don't need stretching so much as you need "warming up" and muscle activation (which you *can* do with some stretches).
- A cardio program will help you to stay steady and keep your heart rate down when the pressure to win cranks up.

- Body weight exercises are more than sufficient for archery.

Steve Ruis

Photo Courtesy of Lloyd Brown

Winning Mental Training

If you expected to read all about the mental tools an archer needs to have at his command here, I am giving you something much more valuable. I will leave descriptions (save the sketchy ones below) to other books. What we need to talk about here is how you build a winning mental program.

Mental Tools for Archers

The most common mental tools used by archers are: positive self-talk, goals (process and outcome), affirmations, and visualization/imagery. Here are short descriptions:

Positive Self-Talk Positive self-talk is simply being positive in all comments you direct at yourself. "I am such an idiot" is an example of negative self-talk. "I can do this!" is an example of positive self-talk. As the old saying goes: "If you think you can or you think you can't . . . you are right."

Goals (Process and Outcome) Goals are obviously something you strive for. The distinction here is that outcome goals are ends in themselves: archers use these to create ladders to success (I want to win that small tournament, then a bigger one, then become state champion, then national champion, . . .). Process goals are goals describing the means to an end, that is to achieve an outcome. For example, "I will have a strong bow arm on every shot of this practice round" is a process goal.

Affirmations Affirmations are statements in which you affirm a certain belief. Repeating these can help generate those beliefs. An example of an affirmation is: "I enjoy the pressure of competition; it means I am close to winning!"

Visualization/Imagery Visualization/Imagery is using one's imagination to help one shoot. This is most often employed during one's shot sequence by imagining a perfect shot just before shooting, and when something rattles you during competition, you can imagine you are shooting at home or in some other comfortable place to calm yourself.

Your Shot Sequence I also include your shot sequence as a mantal tool because it provides a framework not only for the physical shot but for one's mental program also. A shot sequence is the series of steps you undertake to execute a shot. This can be as simple as "#1 Draw, #2 Release" up to having near two dozen steps.

Before we can address mental programming, we need to know a little more about what is being programmed.

The Conscious Mind Trains the Subconscious Mind

A key point in understanding an archery mental program is the distinct roles of the subconscious and conscious "minds." (I put the word "minds" in quotation marks because we still don't understand what a "mind" is; so please understand that much of this is conjecture, but no less useful because of that.) There is a saying that "self-consciousness is the enemy of performance." If you remember what it was like to learn to ride a bicycle or drive a car, you know what I mean. When you are fully engaged consciously with a task with which you are unfamiliar, it is a little like herding cats, very awkward and quite ineffective. But, once you learned those skills, they become subconsciously controlled and practically effortless. Let's look at the roles of these two "minds" in learning repetitive tasks, like shooting arrows.

The Conscious Mind

The conscious mind is basically your thoughts as you are aware of them. Your conscious mind is very limited. You can really only engage one thing at a time consciously, which gives you the ability to concentrate, a very powerful tool. (Typically, though, our greatest strengths also turn out to be weaknesses.) But if we were completely mesmerized by what we are focusing upon, we probably wouldn't have survived long. (What was that noise; was that a Tiger? Hmm.) Because we cannot focus for too long on any one thing and survive, it is normal for our conscious focus to flit around. As an example, focus visually on an object somewhat near you, try to keep your attention, your focus just on that thing. If you picked something large enough that it wasn't entirely included in the cone of focus of your eyes, your eyes probably kept moving to take in the whole object. If you look at something small, you will find it more and more difficult to focus on just that one thing. It is as if your brain is telling you, Okay, I got it; move on; this is dangerous.) You will also notice that all of the other information your eyes are taking in is indistinct. You only can see clearly in about a 10 degree cone. Outside of that cone, all the way out to the limits of your peripheral vision, which can be 180 degrees or more, your vision is not sharp at all. If the object of your interest extends beyond this cone of sharpness, your eyes will flit from one part of it to another to another.

Now, that is not the bad news; this is the bad news: your conscious mind also cannot keep to a single thought for more than about nine seconds. Try it. Imagine a green hot dog, or some other graphic object, and hold it in your mind while somebody times you. When another thought enters your mind, ask for the time and see how long you were able to concentrate. Typically this is less than nine seconds and often much less. Well, at least you now have a reason for why your high school homework bored you. If presented with a problem and you don't get an idea of what to do next, your mind will wander. Studying and all other mental disciplines are about mastering the art of having your mind wander on task and not on to some more pleasant topic.

The Subconscious Mind

For simplicities sake, let's just call the subconscious mind all of your mental abilities which operate when you are unaware of doing them. An excellent example is tying your shoes. What do you think about when tying your shoes? Another example is driving a car. Very little is going on consciously regarding driving. Your subconscious mind seems to be able to deal with a great many things at a much higher speed than you can consciously. This is partly because your subconscious mind is operating about a half of a second ahead of your conscious mind. (Bizarrely, because we think of our conscious mind as the real "us," the subconscious mind operates in our future!)

Here is a comparison of our two "minds" capabilities.

Training Implications Since repetitive tasks are in the province of the subcon-

Your Conscious Mind . . .	Your Subconscious Mind . . .
Can do only one thing at a time.	Can do hundreds of things at a time.
Seems to be your final decision maker.	Strongly influences your decisions.
Has final say in matters of right and wrong.	Whatever. . . .
Tells the subconscious what to learn.	Learns exactly what it is taught.
Acts on information brought up by the subconscious.	Filters out unnecessary information / highlights interesting information.
Is heavily focused on itself.	Can't distinguish between what is real from what is vividly imagined
Is relatively slow.	Is blazing fast.

scious mind, we must train our subconscious minds to do our shooting. The ancient Greeks had a saying that "Repetition is the mother of learning," and this certainly applies to archery, but we need to look at this more carefully. If you were to go to the range every day and put on your headphones and shoot for two hours, would this make you a better archer? The answer is presumed to be "yes," but it is actually "no." You would be a stronger archer as you would develop your archery muscles, but a better archer? Nope.

To train your subconscious mind to make good shots and only good shots, you must focus on what distinguishes a good shot from a bad one. You must let down any shot that deviates from your shot sequence and you must correct any mistake that occurs. The very worst thing that can happen to you is to make a mistake and then have the arrow go into target center. I am sure you have felt that relief when you shot an obviously poor shot that scored well. Fine. Now what? You have just told your subconscious mind that it is okay to improvise as long as the outcome is good! This is bad . . . very bad.

Your subconscious mind has its own agenda. One of its tasks is to keep you alive by husbanding your energy. If any task can be done using less energy, then less food is needed to keep you alive . . . a good thing. Consequently, if you flub up a shot and it required less energy than your normal shot, it is a double whammy; your subconscious mind will be primed to repeat this new, better (meaning "requires less energy") shot. We have learned in just the last few years that the subconscious mind apparently approaches any task as if it were, in some small part, new. (This is for the same reason that you can't focus on just one thing for more than a few seconds; if the subconscious could be perfectly primed to execute the exact same task over and over, predators would learn to trigger the behavior and then, knowing exactly what the response would be, dine on its prey—you.) So, you must reinforce what is a good shot over and over.

Reinforcing what is a good shot is done emotionally. When you shoot a shot well, you must feel good about it. When you shoot a shot poorly, you must disapprove. You do not want these emotions to be strong! Jumping around and "high fiving" people on every good shot will soon exhaust you (and other archer's patience). And feeling strong emotion on a bad shot brings even more attention of your subconscious onto that event. This is a form of imprinting that will actually make that mistake easier to repeat! You need a calm focus on what is and isn't good on each and every shot. This takes the form of calm approval or calm disapproval and each shot must be so reinforced.

So, wearing headphones and listening to music while you are shooting? Not a good idea as that can only distract you and/or cause emotional responses that have nothing to do with the shots you are making. Listening to music you hate is a good drill to learn how to focus in the presence of distractions, but even this is to be done in moderation.

Shooting when you are distracted is bad.

Shooting when you are tired is bad. (Except on a few occasions where doing this can help you learn how to fight through fatigue.)

Because you train your subconscious abilities consciously, and you can concentrate on only one thing at a time, archery practice must focus on only one thing at a time. If you are changing equipment or form or execution . . . you must work on one thing at a time . . . one thing only.

Practice must be sharp and focused on what you are doing and only on what you are doing. Your shot sequence provides a framework for your mental program and you must be focused on executing that continually.

The benefit long term is that once you have built your shot and drilled it home, you will need far less practice to stay sharp than you needed to build your shot in the first place.

What Is a Mental Program?

A mental program is the sum of all of the tools you will use mentally for competition. We will break these down into three sets:

1. tools you use while shooting normally
2. tools you use when things go wrong, and
3. tools you use when planning/preparing.

All of these are needed and the key thing is they are needed now. There is no delay that is acceptable. Too often archers discover mental programs when they are in competition and they are getting beaten and in desperation they think there is some mental hoodoo that will save the day for them. Unfortunately, this is another manifestation of archers believing in magic. There is no mental hoodoo, but there are mental skills which, once learned and if practiced, can make it very much more likely you will have a good day rather than a bad day.

Before we can address the mental tools used when shooting normally, we need to look at the framework that supports all mental programs, the shot sequence.

Shot Sequence Basics

It always astonishes me that students come to me for coaching because they want to learn how to shoot better and they don't use a shot sequence. A *shot sequence*, or as it is sometimes called a *shot routine*, is a series of steps comprising their shot, steps both physical and mental that aid archers a number of ways. Physically a shot sequence assists by providing recognizable segments of the shot to help archers and their coaches analyze and solve form and execution problems. Shot sequences are not confined to just our sport, they are prominent in any precision activity; for example, golfers use them (different ones for putting, tee shots, sand shots, etc.), basketball players (but only at the free throw line as far as I can tell), rifle shooters, and so forth.

While a basic archery shot sequence, which may be from four to twenty-four steps (these are only the shortest and longest I have heard of), is usually introduced as a physical aid, the mental aspects are as valuable or possibly even more valuable.

One of the first shot sequences I had ever heard of was the "Nine Steps to the Ten Ring" which some say was created by Julia Bowers, others say by Ruth Rowe, and still others by . . . others. (It's hard to give credit when people don't put their names on things!) The nine steps in this sequence are:

1. Stand
2. Nock
3. Set
4. Pre-draw
5. Draw
6. Anchor
7. Aim
8. Release
9. Followthrough

Please accept the fact that variations in the words and numbers of steps occur. And there has been so much confusion over what a "pre-draw" is that the term is rapidly disappearing. The problem I have had since I first saw the Nine Steps is that the list is more than a little opaque. Here is the way I present the list now:

1. Take Your Stance
2. Nock an Arrow
3. Set Your Hands
4. Raise the Bow
5. Draw
6. Find Your Anchor
7. Aim
8. Release the String
9. Follow Through.

This list uses short phrases that are more indicative of what is being done. But, if you don't like either of these you are free to make up your own lists and own terms. My shot sequence when I shoot my compound bow has 13 steps (14 now that I am working on a problem with my bow hand).

A key element of any shot sequence is a visualization of a perfect shot. I do this before I raise the bow (after Step 3 and before Step 4 in the list above). This is because I am ready to shoot once my hands are set and a shot only takes a few seconds. The visualization takes several seconds so there is no time to do it later in the shot, and the whole purpose of doing it is as a rehearsal, so doing it later makes no sense. In my sequence, this is an actual step, but it can be part of a "set your hands" step also. What this provides is that at least every other shot is a perfect shot (albeit many are imaginary) and these shots imprint the subconscious mind with the task needed. (Remember that your subconscious mind can't distinguish between what is real and what is vividly imagined.)

The Mental Side of a Shot Sequence

Archery is a kinesthetic sport, meaning it is all about how a shot feels. But human beings don't seem to be focused on what they feel. In fact, being "touchy-feely" is a disparaging term used in jokes. Our minds get between us and physical reality in that we "interpret" our physical sensations in ways that are counterproductive in archery. This is where training is really needed and a good coach's help is very valuable.

Ultimately, the shot sequence steps are interlaced with a strong mental program. For each physical step of the shot sequence there is a mental check list and this gives the mind (both conscious (earlier) and subconscious (later)) something to do, something that won't distract or intrude on the shot. Each step also provides a touch point, a point in time where certain physical sensations are checked. In the long run, archers become more in tune with the feel of good shots to be able to distinguish them from bad ones.

So, here are what I ask archers to focus on in their shot sequence. (I am using the Nine Steps applied to a recurve archer shooting a high anchor as a model.)

Shot Sequence Step	Mental Check
1. Take Your Stance	feet shoulder width apart, toes on line to target, everything relaxed
2. Nock an Arrow	See arrow on rest, cock vane out, hear snap of nock (maybe clicker in position)
3. Set Your Hands	(bow) on pad of thumb, knuckles at 45°/(draw) thumb and little finger tucked out of the way, deep hook, everything else relaxed
4. Raise Your Bow	bow shoulder stays down, bow elbow rotated out, draw elbow up, hands stay put/relaxed
5. Draw	pull is smooth and crisp with draw elbow up
6. Find Your Anchor	thumb under jaw, press the flesh (high anchor)
7. Aim	focus on the point you want to hit (or aim at)
8. Release the String	let the string go, don't let go of the string (finger release)
9. Follow Through	hold form until the bow finishes it's bow (the other bow)

All of these checkpoints are both visual and tactile, and they allow a new archer to focus on what they are supposed to feel at each stage of the shot. They have to feel most of them because they are really hard to see.

The key mental aspect is: *if anything, anything at all—mental or physical—intrudes from the environment or a prior step, you must let down and start over.* This I call the Rule of Discipline. You cannot become a winning archer without following this rule. Essentially this rule says that you will only shoot shots you *know* are good shots. Shooting shots you *hope* are good will not get you into the winner's circle. Shooting shots you know are bad will require you to shoot many good shots to wash away their influence, a tremendous waste of effort.

Tools You Use While Shooting Normally

Here are mental tools that you can use while shooting and competing normally. You are familiar, I am sure, with some of the things that can go wrong. One of these that all archers learn the hard way is thinking about score: if while competing you start thinking about your score, your potential score is about to go down. The reason is that thinking about score is a distraction that won't help you focus on executing good shots. The things your conscious mind is supposed to focus on is replaced by the topic of "score" instead and . . . oops, "I just shot a 3!" Winning scores require mental focus. You must concentrate on just what is needed to make good shots while shooting. Your ally here is the Rule of Discipline. If you follow this rule, in both practice and competition, you will have embraced a tool which will accelerate your learning how to win more than any other. So, avoiding thinking about score is a kind of mental tool.

Self-Talk Normally self-talk comes in when you are shooting fine and everything is going swimmingly and then some negative thought pops into your head, a thought such as when looking through your binoculars, you see a shot just low enough to be out of the top scoring ring and "Whoa, here we go again!" pops into your head. Maybe the shot is "in" or maybe it is "out" but one shot does not indicate a trend. A positive piece of self-talk to replace the above might be "I didn't expect to be perfect in this round and it is always a good sign when my misses are by tiny amounts. And I may have caught it outside-in, anyway."

Negative thoughts are pounded into our heads from the minute we are born and can't be expected to just stop when we are shooting. When negative thoughts happen to you, you need to take a mental break and then rewrite that negative as a positive thought and think it to yourself with conviction.

Process Goals If you are working on an aspect of your form which needs shoring up, you may need a "shot thought" much as golfers use. One that I have used is "strong bow arm" when I was having a bow shoulder problem. I had a process goal of having that shot thought just before aiming. After each end, I wrote down how many of the shots in that end included the shot thought of "strong bow arm." In this way, the process goal is reinforced each and every end so it doesn't get forgotten in the heat of competition. I can't say this strongly enough, if you have a process goal, you must evaluate each shot and make a written record of "how you did" at the end of each end of shooting. It is not enough just to have a goal, it must be evaluated continually to provide the focus the goal needs to succeed. (This is how you learn to train yourself!)

Visualizations As mentioned above, most people use visualizations or imagery to implant in their minds what a good shot looks like and feels like (and sounds like, etc.; the more senses involved in the imagining, the better) before they shoot every shot on the belief that it is easier to repeat a complex task than do it from scratch. This is based on the idea that the subconscious mind cannot distinguish between what is real and what is vividly imagined.

Tools You Use When Things Go Wrong

Here is where you earn your wings. What happens when you shoot a shot and you expected a 10 and got a 6? That is, what happens when things go wrong? As I have said before, there are three possible sources of a bad shot:

a. the external environment (wind, birds, etc.)

b. your equipment, and/or

c. you

Well, which was it . . . the source of that 6? This is the archer's problem.

Rational Troubleshooting When trying to decipher a "bad shot," if you allow your emotions to take over, you lose. You have only so much time to figure out what went wrong and correct it for the next shot. Spending time getting upset and then calming yourself back down doesn't solve the problem.

The first thing I do is mentally replay the shot in my mind. Did I try to "help" the shot and push it over into the 6-ring? Did I drop my bow arm? What questions get asked depends on whether the shot was high, low, left, or right. If high, left, or right I certainly am not going to check to see if a dropped bow arm was responsible as that would account only for a low shot. To do this accurately, I need to have a short list of things to check for each direction of misses (see diagram next page).

But winning archers don't have generic lists, their lists include the cause of such shots based only upon what *they* are likely to do. So, start taking notes if you haven't already.

If my "instant replay" of my shot doesn't indicate a reason for the problem, I next check for environmentals. If there is a wind flag, which direction is it blowing? Did the wind gust during the shot? Does that account for the problem? And so on.

If not, I then check over my equipment, looking for loose arrow rests, loose sight blocks, something that would cause the problem. I do this last because I have checked, double checked, then triple checked my equipment to make sure it wouldn't fail, plus I am sensitive to things being "different" about my equipment.

If none of these come up with a cause of the problem, I have to put the problem out of my mind and shoot another shot. If I don't put the last shot out of mind, thinking about it will probably mess up my next shot and I will get neither a good score nor the information I need to continue.

Do not think you will be able to solve every problem! Consider the following scenario. I was shooting in the Pacific Coast Championship at 70m. After shooting one shot, I couldn't spot the arrow with my spotting scope, but because I was shooting second line and the other archers were quite good, there were quite a few arrows packed into the center. Since I was mostly in the center myself, I assumed that my arrow was hiding with the others in one of the clumps. When we got down to the target, I had a score of 5 arrows for 47 points! Where was my 6th arrow? I found it in the grass behind the target, but there was just no way I had shot that arrow so low! When I pulled the arrow out of the grass I found the problem—the arrow had no point in it. Even in September, that venue had quite a high temperature and apparently, the friction from the previous shot had loosened up the hot melt glue holding in the arrow's point and the point remained in the target butt when I pulled it the previous end. (You may well imagine that it is now part of my routine that when I pull my arrows I check to make sure all of them still have their points. So many lessons are learned the hard way.) And, if I had noticed that very low shot and done anything to "correct" for what I had "done wrong," my score would have been even lower!

You must learn to troubleshoot "bad shots" in such a way that you can minimize the damage. If you are lucky enough that a bad shot only costs you a few points and it is relatively early, you can catch up to a winning score. If it is late and very costly,

Arrows Hitting High
- nocking point too low
- bow "heeled"
- draw elbow too high
- bow drawn too far
- jerking up on release
- sight set wrong

Arrows Hitting Left
- aiming with wrong eye
- arrows too stiff
- floating anchor
- arrow slid off rest
- string hit armguard
- sight set wrong

Arrows Hitting Right
- arrows too weak
- bow canted (w/sight)
- pushed bow right
- plucking string
- sight set wrong

Arrows Hitting Low
- bow arm dropped
- nocking point too high
- arrow fell off of rest
- string hit armguard
- arrow nocked above locator
- sight set wrong

Switch the Left and Right reasons for a left-handed archer.

you will probably be "out of luck." Sometimes, those are the breaks of the game.

Visualizations What if the poor shot is due to one of the things you tend to do wrong? You have just executed incorrectly, now what? If you focus on what you did wrong, it just makes it more likely that you will repeat that incorrect execution.

First, think about what you do when you flub tying your shoelaces. Do you go back through the steps, walking through them methodically? No, you merely focus a bit more on the task at hand, that is you avoid distracting thoughts or activities and then you simply tie your shoe. This is what you must do in archery also. You must focus on making a good shot a bit more. Very important in this is to imagine a good shot in your normal sequence especially vividly. You must not "try harder" or any other foolishness. When you have tense moments, your response needs to be to relax, not to tense up even more as a form of "trying harder."

A special case of this are folks who start tournaments weakly. The first 2-3 shots are shaky at best and then they settle down to shoot as they are capable. If you are in this category there is a visualization exercise you can use to avoid this problem. The drill is to mentally shoot the first two ends and include walking to the target and scoring perfect ends in your visualization. When the first scoring end comes, it will be as if you were on your third end and past your nervous zone. Some people use practice ends for this purpose (when these apply), shooting them as if they were scoring. Both of these techniques can work . . . if you practice them so they are available when competing.

Affirmations If you use affirmations, a good time to repeat the pertinent ones is between a bad shot and your next shot. If these help at all, it is a good time to receive such positive reinforcement.

Have A Recovery Strategy Having a "recovery routine" is a good strategy. Here is an example of what you must do: first, you must stop thinking about the mistake. You must think about something else: a green hot dog, an Orc ballerina, anything as long as it is different from the poor shot you just made. Next, you must do something physical, like jostling the arrows in your quiver or tapping your bow or resettling your binoculars, something physical that gets you out of the realm of the entirely mental, then you need to begin the process of engaging the next shot. If you use "cue words" like: "strong bow arm" or "like a butterfly" such cues can get you mentally into the next shot. According to Troy Bassham of Mental Management Systems (*www.mentalmanagement.com*), this process needs to take at least seven seconds, so don't just rush into your next shot thinking it will wipe away the memory of the bad shot with the image of a good one. Resetting mentally takes a bit of time. When things go wrong, execute your strategy and get back on track.

Recovery Practice I recommend to all my students that they start every shooting session with two things: a couple of let downs (as a reminder that letting down is always an option) and by shooting their shot deliberately and about 10% slower than they normally would. The second activity is a first-stage physical recover program. When you need a recovery program, don't you want to have practiced it just a little while ago? (The shooting warm up continues from the slightly slower, deliberate shots to more flowing shots at normal tempo.)

What we are doing right now is thinking about things you do not want to think about—what happens when things go wrong. But if you don't do it now, you will be stuck doing it every time something does go wrong. So, spend some time developing and practicing your recovery routine. It will give you something positive and constructive to do when things do go wrong.

Tools You Use When Planning/Preparing

Several of your mental tools are useful in planning and preparing, in fact, you would profit from considering planning to be a mental tool itself. Since we specifically address planning elsewhere (see Chapter 8), I am going to just discuss two useful mental tools here.

Outcome Goals Let's say your goal for the season is to place in the top ten in the USAA Outdoor Nationals at the end of the summer. From the Internet you consider that a FITA Round score of 1300 would be sufficient to guarantee that placing. If your current FITA Round score is 1220, what should your goal be? If you answered 1300, you have some work to do! You have to ask yourself when was the last time you got a 80 point improvement in your average score on this round. (Answer: probably never.) When you set goals, they need to be clear and achievable. Maybe your first goal is to get your average score to 1240. Then maybe to 1260, 1280, and finally to 1300. These goals make a "ladder to success."

A goal of 1240 when you already shoot a 1220 sounds easy enough, but what are you going to do to make that change? If it were all that easy, wouldn't you have done it already? Ah, here is the rub. You now have to figure out what you will be doing differently to make a 20 point difference in your average score.

If you sit down with your coach and a pad and pen, you can probably come up with a list of things. Then you have to start trying them and see which of them actually make improvements. The process we will talk about later but for now, which feeling will you rather have:

    a. I only have another 20 points to make my goal of 1300, but I met the 1240 goal, and the 1260 goal, and the 1280 goal; I can make this one, too! or

    b. I only have another 20 points to make my goal of 1300, but I have had this goal all summer and I am running out of time; I am not going to make it.

Working your way up a ladder, one rung at a time, rather than trying to make one giant leap, provides you with a series of successes that enables you to gauge your progress as well as convince you that you can meet your goals.

Affirmations Affirmations can be written on 3x5 cards and stashed around your house or apartment (on your dresser, on the mirror in your bathroom, on the fridge, etc.). Every time you encounter a card, you stop and read it (out loud is best). This guarantees that these positive thoughts about the "you" you want to become are reinforced several times a day. (If you want an inspiring story involving affirmations, look up Billy Mills' story of how he got his Olympic Gold Medal in the 10,000 meter race.)

Planning tools are almost entirely mental and are a great help in getting you onto the winner's platform.

Mental Practice

I have heard the question often: "When should I practice the mental part?" The answer is that the mental and physical are inseparable, at least the "normal shooting" part. The mental tools you use when planning are obviously used every time you do any planning. The only mental tools that get separate practice are the "tools you use when things go wrong." Obviously you can't wait for things to go wrong (even though they seem to often enough) for opportunities to practice. At a bare minimum, I will go though my "disaster tool kit" whenever I am preparing for a tournament. Coaches can help but creating "problems" in the middle of practice sessions and requiring you to adjust ("Your bowstring (or D-Loop, or . . .) just broke. You have fifteen minutes to repair the problem and get sighted back in.").

As a general rule, you can't prepare for all eventualities. I remember a tournament I had prepared for and thought about for months. I had done everything to virtually guarantee I would shoot a personal best (in fact I considered it a foregone conclusion). I just neglected to inform the deer which ran out in front of my truck, not 300 yards from home. The deer ran away from the collision but I limped home, hoping to get my truck repaired so I could get to work on Monday.

While I was writing this chapter, we had an indoor club shoot. The best shooter in this area ended up arriving without his quiver or his release aids. He had changed cars at the last minute and hadn't gotten everything transferred. After suffering the usual teasing from his mates, he proceeded to borrow a floor quiver and one of the several release aids offered that he checked during practice to find one to use during the competition. He shot the whole round with one of the borrowed releases and while his X-count suffered a little, he shot his normal perfect score. This is a fine example of mental practice. Instead of going home or just watching, this archer used the opportunity to practice his disaster routines. Using unfamiliar equipment can be disconcerting, but it is easier the second time than the first and the third is easier than the second. There is a reason this guy is the top archer in the region and building up his mental toughness is one aspect of that.

You should be able to anticipate common weather events (wind, rain, etc.) and be prepared for them both physically and mentally. And if something comes up you couldn't prepare for, well, probably no one else could either, so you are no worse off with regard to winning.

Getting There vs. Being There

The last couple of your practice scores were right there, high enough to win the tournament you are focusing on. Are you ready? Maybe yes, maybe no; you see your performance is largely controlled by your self image. Your self image is a subconscious part of you that can be likened to a definition of who you are. Your self image is intimately linked to your chances of winning. To explain this, consider two archers showing up at a major tournament: one is relaxed, confident, and is telling everyone he is shooting really, really well because he is; the other is tense, worried, and is telling everyone about his struggles. Which of these two guys has the better chance of winning? Duh. The confident guy. But, if the guy was faking all the confident behavior and talk: he isn't shooting all that well, the confidence and relaxed postures are all an act, then all bets are off.

The real winners appear confident and relaxed because they are confident and relaxed. They have a high expectation of winning because winning is something they do; they are winners. Their internal picture of themselves, their self-image, is that of a winner. These guys have a real edge.

So, how are you supposed to get this self image, without a lot of experience winning? Well, for one, you can't get by lying to yourself or anyone else. You must first convince yourself that you can be expected to shoot winning scores any time you want. So, how many of those potentially winning practice scores do you need to create this winning self-image? Well, let me tell you a story about that. When I lived in California, my archery club had a weekly indoor league shoot at an archery shop every winter. I was still learning how to shoot compound unlimited/freestyle and one of these leagues used the NFAA five-spot target to shoot a 300 round. I started out this session shooting 296, 297, 296, 297, 298, and 298. So, the next six-week league I stuck to the same target, because I was really feeling I was "getting it" and I wanted to shoot a 300. So the next league started 298, 299, 298, 299, and 300! Cool! I even had 42 X's which was a new personal best X-count for me. Now, can you guess what my next score was? It was a 286. Talk about a smack down. I thought I had arrived. A fellow club member hadn't shot anything but 300 on that round for over ten years. His self image was one that was telling him that he was a "300 shooter." My self image at that point was of a guy who got lucky and shot one 300 in his entire life.

Here's the thing. We all have comfort zones associated with our performances. If we are performing way below what our self image is, we tend to get a little upset with ourselves and bear down and we perform better. I am sure you have experienced this. On the flip side, if we are shooting "lights out," way over our heads, something almost always happens to bring us down . . . down and back into our comfort zone, the one that includes shooting scores like that. It is close to being a form of personal sabotage. If you haven't experienced this before, just check out the performance of any pro golfer who has never won a tournament and is leading on the last day of a tournament. On very, very rare occasions, these newbies win. Much more often, though, they drop down the rankings like a stone. It is even worse when their playing partner on the final round is Tiger Woods (the Tiger Woods of 2009 and earlier). You can't count on him making more mistakes than you do. And, gee, performing in front of these huge crowds is so different. And they are all cheering for him. Do you think those golfers include "Tiger Hunter" as some part of their self images? I would guess not.

When I learned about comfort zones, I thought back to the string of scores I described above. Before shooting the perfect score, I could remember making my first miss in several of those rounds and having felt *relieved*! The tension of trying not to miss had ended; I was relieved. This was more like me! But, argh! I didn't want that to be "just like me."

So, how do you change your self image to include you being capable of shooting winning scores? This is actually not that hard. Here is a technique I have heard from Coach Len Cardinale, Coach Bernie Pellerite, and Coaches Lanny and Troy

Bassham of Mental Management Systems. Let's say the goal is to become a consistent shooter of 300 scores on the NFAA 300 Indoor Round. You start with a five spot target set up at just five yards distance. Set your sight appropriately and shoot five arrows, aiming for the center of the X-ring but keeping your focus on shooting with good form and execution. Shoot the next five arrows. Now, if you miss the X-ring (or the spot, you can choose the level of the exercise), you must start over, from the beginning on a new target face. When you have shot 60 perfect X's (or spots), at your next practice you must do it again. After you have shot 3-5 perfect rounds this way, you can move the target out a couple of yards and repeat the drill. After you have shot 3-5 consecutive perfect rounds at that distance, you can move the target out to 10 yards and repeat the drill. Keep shooting and moving the target back until you are at regulation distance.

There are several variations of this drill. You can start with overlarge targets. You can use different distances. The key elements to keep in any variation is the building upon success and the "do over" requirements. When you have gotten back to the formal competition distance and formal target size and have shot 3-5 perfect scores, you will also have shot dozens of perfect scores. You will be quite used to shooting perfect scores. You will be quite used to shooting arrows into the X-ring.

The point is to shoot perfectly you must start at a distance at which this is easy and prove to yourself you can do it, become comfortable with doing it consistently. Then stretch out the difficulty just a bit and do it some more. This does work; I recommend it to you. Use caution, though, if you can't shoot 300 or close to 300 already, this is asking too much from a simple process.

So, will your self image change through such a regimen? The answer is yes. Can it still be improved? The answer is yes. You have yet to prove to yourself that you *consistently* shoot 300 under tournament conditions, while traveling and eating fast food, etc. But to become a consistent winner, you have to win and to win you have to believe you can. Proving you can shoot arrow after arrow in the center of your target to yourself is the first part of this journey.

Mental Traps

I can't end this chapter without warning you about some mental traps that archers can fall prey to. They are based in the psychological phenomena called cognitive dissonance and confirmation bias.

Cognitive Dissonance As with all things psychologic, there is no "proof" of the existence of anything, but the concept of cognitive dissonance seems to ring true. Cognitive dissonance is just that whenever we hold two incompatible beliefs at the same time, we will distort one or the other or both so that they can live together. A common example is people who claim the world is coming to an end on Thursday and release a statement on Friday indicating that they knew what was going to happen all along. The classic example in archery is when you attend a competition thinking you have a good chance to win even though your scores aren't really good enough. The dissonance is set up around the typical winning score, let's say a score of 540 in an NFAA Field Round, and the fact that your average score is around 510. The odds of you shooting 30+ points over your average are vanishingly small. This is proven by the fact that you shot only one score over 530 in the last ten years. So, the vast majority of your scores are sub 540, but you will fixate on that 539 you shot, thinking "It could win for me!" You pay no attention to the "the 506 score I shot last week will lose for me" thoughts. You can delude yourself to the degree that when you lose, you will feel disappointed. In reality, you had no realistic chance of winning.

Whenever two thoughts clash with one another (basically both can't be true; they are incompatible: "the world will end on Thursday—the world did not end on Thursday") everyone tends to bridge the gap between those thoughts until they are compatible.

Confirmation Bias Confirmation bias was described in a song by Paul Simon ("The Boxer") in which he wrote "still the man hears what he wants to hear and disregards the rest. . . ." We're that man! Once we have bought a new bow, or made any other major purchase, we don't want to feel that we have made a bad decision or have wasted our money, so when we hear something good about what we bought, that sticks in our mind. If something bad about our new bow is said, it slides through our minds like an otter through water or we contest the information (That can't be true; you misheard the guy!). This is normal human behavior and it applies to archery in small and large ways. For example, a dear friend was told she had a good finger release. She liked hearing this and even repeated it herself. Consequently no work was done to make her release any better or even different. Comments to the contrary were not heard. Finally, high-speed video showed that her release was a dead release followed by a beautiful, although fake, followthrough of the release hand.

More commonly, people invest a great deal of money in bows or arrows or whatever and then only hear things that confirm their good judgment and certainly nothing about the object's shortcomings. Obviously you can't compensate for shortcomings if you don't know what they are.

You need to be aware of these general human tendencies as they apply to your archery. A major reason that you need to make written records and do actual tests to see if changes in your form, execution, or equipment really made improvements, as it is very easy to fall prey to what psychologists call the Hawthorne Effect. Basically, the *Hawthorne Effect* is that anything done with the goal of making things better will actually make things better . . . for a short time. This was discovered over 50 years ago in a study of office work conditions. In that study office workers were told that a change was being made in office lighting that should make their work easier. Lo and behold, after the lighting was brightened just a bit, productivity increased. Then they were told that another adjustment should make things even better and the lights were dimmed back to their original level. Dumbfounded the researchers observed another productivity increase! This almost sounds too good to be true but reality reasserts itself in that the effects are gone in just a few days and things go back to normal.

Here's how the Hawthorne Effect applies to you. How many times have you gotten a new archery gizmo and decided within a day or even an hour or so that those new arrows, that new bow, etc. made a real improvement in your shooting. Well, they/it may have but it may also have lasted only a day or so. So, after you have gotten used to your new thingamabob, you need to do a group test or standard round test (or tests!) to see if there is any real improvement or whether you are just deluding yourself.

Written records are your ally in this! If you think you have made just so much progress but you look back a year or two and find out that your scores haven't really changed, you have a way to really tell what is going on. Your memory is always susceptible to cognitive dissonance and confirmation bias and it cannot be trusted.

Target Panic . . . Shussh!

I can't let this chapter end without saying something about *target panic*. Target panic is the scourge of archers, a mental affliction that in severe cases can convince one of the reality of demonic possession. Some people won't even use the term out loud.

Target panic is a mental condition that inhibits the ability to execute a shot. In extreme cases archers freeze at full draw and can't let go of the string. Or they can't get their sight's aperture anywhere near the target center. Others shot uncontrolably when the first see the target, yet are nowhere near the target center.

And, the fact is, that most people encounter target panic, usually in some mild form, along the way. Because there have been no serious studies of this affliction I devoted four chapters (four!) in my book "More on Coaching Archery." The upshot is: target panic is curable, usualy by reprogramming one's shot. I have had it. Many, many others have, too. It is curable. So, if you find yourself, all of a suden, unable to execute your shot normally and, no matter what you try, it doesn't seem to get better, don't quit, get help! Reprogramming your shot can take as little as a few weeks and you will be back executing successful shots.

Sidebar—The Capstone of a Mental Program
One of the most important aspects of an archer's mental program is that which allows him or her to always shoot in rhythm. Some archers shoot quickly, some shoot slowly. Fast archers who try to shoot slowly or slow archers who try to shoot quickly will only find disappointment. I am convinced that whatever your rhythm is, it is what it is and trying to change it is a fool's errand. You need to shoot in your rhythm. The task is becoming consistent at your particular rhythm.

Finding Your Rhythm This is the hard part. You either need to have someone with a stopwatch help you or possibly you can use a metronome to figure it out. In the stopwatch approach, you have somebody time how many seconds (without you noticing them doing it) it takes from raising your bow to releasing the string (or any two well defined points, with your shot between them). After each shot, you say "yes" if the shot felt good and was in rhythm or "no" if it didn't feel good or was out of rhythm.

After recording the times and arrow scores of many dozens of shots from more than one session, you try to correlate the number of seconds to the quality of the shot. One way to do this is to enter the number of seconds, arrow scores, and the yes's and no's into a three-column spread sheet, sort the rows for time and see if the yes's cluster around any particular shot time. Do the good arrow scores cluster around any particular shot time? Do the good scores correlate with the "yes" ratings? (In this you are asking the question: "Am I a good judge of whether I am in rhythm?") For the sake of this discussion, let's say that most of the yes's and good arrow scores were from 4-6 seconds. This, then is an indicator of your shot rhythm and there are now a number of ways to lock in that rhythm (see below).

The metronome approach to finding your rhythm is to play a metronome and count off your shot, so many "clicks" for each step of the shot sequence. (The numbers will vary because the steps are not the same length.) If the metronome is set too fast, you will feel rushed or unable to count fast enough. If it is set too slow, you will feel sluggish and impatient. Eventually you get it set right and then you have found the rhythm you want to lock in. This can be confirmed by arrow scores shot at various test rhythms: the best rhythm should produce the better scoring arrows.

Locking in Your Rhythm There are a couple of ways to lock in your personal shot rhythm. One way is through feedback. Again, you need somebody with a stop watch. If your slice of time is 4-6 seconds from raising to bow to loose, your helper practices with you and times each shot. If you shoot quicker than the four seconds, he tells you. If you reach 6 seconds before shooting, he announces "let down" and you must let down the string. The feedback eventually gets you to shoot in your best rhythm. You will need several sessions to do this and you may need to test yourself at intervals to check on your status.

Another method is to use a personal metronome (they clip on to your ear) and practice in your rhythm. You can't necessary use it in competitions, though (check your organization's rules).

Yet another method is you may have a snippet of music in your head that is in the same tempo as your shot rhythm (or you may hear it and recognize it then). A great many archers use a sample of a song as part of their shot sequence. It helps them to stay in rhythm.

Sidebar—Mind Games and Trash Talking

There are competitors who will try to throw you off your game by playing mind games: disrupting your thinking, your pre-competition routine, arguing with you over a shooting lane on the practice field, etc. As much as possible you do not want to engage these people in any of their shenanigans. The reason is there is no upside, nothing to gain for you. I once asked Rick McKinney whether he or Darrel Pace, who were winning everything in Olympic-style archery in the 70's and 80's, ever engaged in mind games. His response was "no" in that he wanted his competitors to know they couldn't beat him, even on their best days. That is a kind of arrogance I can support.

It is somewhat traditional during friendly competitions to engage in a little "trash talking." For example, at one of our club's shoots a member brought with him a medal for a friend that he had picked up for him. When presenting him with his second place medal he said, "If you want to see what the first place medal looks like, I can show you mine. Have you ever seen one?" Now, this was all good natured ribbing between friends, but it can become harder edged when the competition gets a little hotter. I recommend that you do not engage in trash talking . . . while you are shooting. Save up your really good material for meals or meetings, etc. It is much too easy to let such talk get under your skin, causing you to lose your focus while shooting. Just turn away from such comments and get into your routines.

Key Points
Chapter 6 Winning Mental Training

You will need to read about mental tools for archers elsewhere. Here I focus on building a winning mental program.

- The most common mental tools used by archers are: positive self-talk, goals (process and outcome), affirmations, and visualization/imagery.
- Self-consciousness is the enemy of performance.
- The subconscious mind can't distinguish between what is real and what is vividly imagined.
- The conscious mind trains the subconscious mind.
- To train your subconscious mind to make good shots and only good shots, you must focus on what distinguishes a good shot from a bad one.

- You must reinforce what is a good shot over and over.
- Reinforcing what is a good shot is done emotionally, basically through a feeling satisfaction attached to that shot.
- Because you train your subconscious abilities consciously, and you can concentrate on only one thing at a time, archery practice must focus on only one thing at a time.
- Your shot sequence provides a framework for your mental program and you must be focused on executing that continually.
- A mental program is the sum of all of the tools you will use mentally for competition.
- During a shot, if anything, anything at all—mental or physical—intrudes from a prior step or from the environment, you must let down and start over (the *Rule of Discipline*).
- Self-talk, what you say *to* yourself *about* yourself, must always be positive.
- Negative self-talk can be banished by turning it into positive self-talk.
- Process goals and their evaluation help you become better.
- Perfect shot visualizations that immediately precede each shot help you execute good shots.
- Winning archers have a mental list including the common causes of their bad shots to use when troubleshooting bad shots.
- There are three possible sources of a bad shot: a. the external environment, b. your equipment, and/or c. you; the real question is "Which was it this time?"
- When you make a bad shot you must focus on making a good shot a bit more. You must never "try harder" or any other foolishness.
- Having a "recovery routine" to follow after bad shots is a good strategy.
- You must spend some time thinking about things you do not want to think about—what happens when things go wrong. This will help you "find your shot" when it is lost faster than anything else.
- Use outcome goals to create "ladders to success" which get you used to being successful.
- Mental tools require practice as much as physical tools.
- Winners have a self image of being a winner and self image determines performance. To become a consistent winner, you have to be a winner. (Yes, it is a paradox.)
- When you are performing much worse or much better that you are accustomed to, you will bring yourself up or down into your comfort zone.
- You can change your self image and comfort zone through dedicated practice.
- There are mental traps you can fall into and learning about them can help you avoid them.
- Shooting in rhythm is the final mental aspect of refining your shot and making it regular and dependable.

Steve Ruis

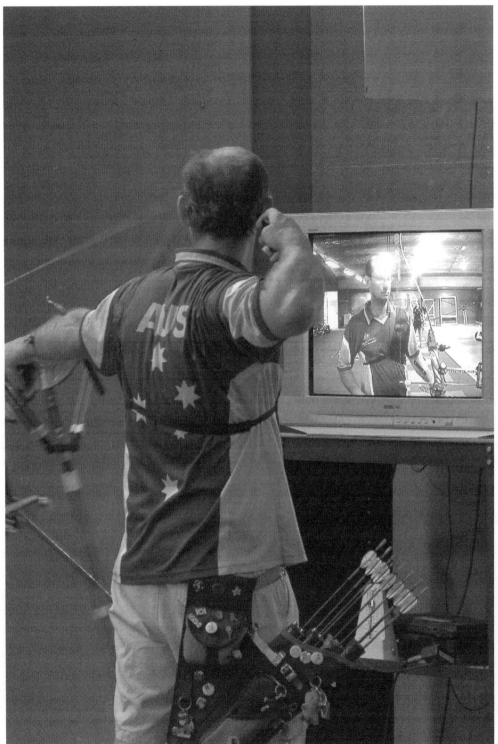

Photo Courtesy of Andy Macdonald

7

Winning Practice

I had originally decided not to include this chapter. The reason was that you will find things that impact how you need to practice in every one of the other chapters. In the equipment chapter, there are recommendations regarding testing new or different equipment . . . during practice time. During the mental skills chapter there are recommendations about introducing and using mental skills . . . during practice time. During the planning chapter there are recommendations about how to plan what you are to do . . . during practice time. So, I felt this chapter unnecessary. Obviously I changed my mind.

This chapter is short with the simple goals of a) providing a single focus for the topic of practice and b) to lay out my philosophy of practice.

Practice Is . . .

Practice is . . . all kinds of things. As an example, one of my most successful practices took just a few minutes. I drove to the range, unpacked, stretched a little and stepped up to the 60 yard target on the practice range. I set my sight for 60 yards, drew and released—X. The next arrow—X. The third arrow—X. I checked each of these outcomes with binoculars and after the third arrow I walked to the target and verified that, indeed, all three shots had been solidly in the X-ring. I packed up and went home. I spent more time driving back and forth than I did in practice.

To make sense of this you need to know the purpose of that practice session. All I wanted from that practice session was a confirmation of my marks and that I was "ready" for a competition that was occurring in just a couple of days. I already had checked (and double-checked) my marks and my equipment. I just wanted confirmation that I was prepared. That close to a competition was not the time to be fiddling with my equipment, shooting high numbers of arrows, or fine-tuning my technique.

I tell you this story not as some sort of a brag, but as an example of the principle that *each practice must have reasons for its existence*. If you don't know why you are practicing, specifically, you are probably wasting your time and quite probably deluding yourself.

Here is my philosophy on archery practices.

A Practice Philosophy

Some of this is backed up with science, much of it is based on my experience and the experiences of much better archers. (I always listen to my betters.)

Don't Practice Doing It Wrong If your shot isn't right, don't spend a lot of time on repetition ("volume" shooting, practice scores, etc.). All you will be doing is making it harder to make changes, changes you already know you need! Think about it; if the Rule of Discipline (If anything, anything at all—mental or physical—intrudes from a prior step or from your environment, you must let down and start over.) exists because you don't want to shoot a *single* shot incorrectly, in competition or practice, why would you want to spend whole practice sessions drilling so you could shoot incorrectly?

If there are things wrong with your shot, you need to fix them. The criterion is always that all aspects (steps, parts, etc.) of your shot should be about the same quality. If you have weak points—fix them!

Every Practice Must Have a Plan If you go to practice without a plan of what you want to accomplish, you are up against the old saying "if you believe you can or you believe you can't, either way you are right." Just "flinging arrows" can be labeled practice, but it may actually be counterproductive. You need to be doing what it is you really need to be doing, and it requires some thought ahead of time to identify that. I recommend you write it down. Your plan doesn't have to be complicated, it might just be a list of two or three things. Here's an example:

1. bare shaft test new arrows
2. rope bow drill with release aid
3. shoot practice 300 round

Do yourself a favor and take practice seriously and see what happens. This is what the top pros do. They do nothing haphazardly.

The Right Amount of Practice is the Right Amount I do not believe that practicing for a set number of shots (100 shots, 400 shots, etc.) or for a set time (an hour, four hours, seven days a week, etc.) can be right, let alone is right. These are totally arbitrary markers and meeting them cannot be indicative of the accomplishment of anything. To determine if you have had a successful practice (or not) requires you to know what it was you were trying to accomplish. This is why throughout this book there are so many references to how to measure what you are doing. Sometimes the measure is a feeling: the quality of the feel of your shot, for example. If my "three X practice" outcome had been accomplished through three poorly shot arrows, I would not have packed up and left. What I accomplished was three quality shots with three quality outcomes requiring no sight setting tweakings, etc. That was the basis for my decision that "practice was over."

If you have a practice plan and what you were trying to accomplish is complete, you are done. If you want to continue shooting "for fun" that is fine, it just isn't "practice" you are doing.

You Need an Outside Point of View Archery's history is riddled with examples of archers going it alone. Let's face it, it is flat out much easier to just do it yourself.

You don't have to coordinate schedules, reserve shooting space, etc. At the same time there are testimonials to the value that a good coach or shooting partner can provide. Archery, as a sport, has not had a tradition of coaching anything at all like other sports do. Every baseball player, football player, tennis player, or golfer has had extensive coaching from coaches trained in their sport. Archery . . . not so much so, but maybe that is changing. It is my opinion that a shooting partner is better than nothing and that having training partners is a good thing, but not as good as having a quality coach working with you. In fact, I will go so far to claim that the lack of quality coaching is the prime cause of resorting to shooting partners in lieu of having a coach.

Whether you are able to secure the services of a quality coach or find a helpful shooting partner, you do need some kind of outside viewpoint. Maybe the ready availability of video cameras (even with HS/very slow motion now) and the ability to send video clips around the country via the Internet will help fill the coaching vacuum, but some kind of educated outside viewing is absolutely necessary.

The Battle is Always Against Self-Delusion I would be tremendously embarrassed to tell you how many competitions I went to with the goal of winning that I had zero (zero!) chance of winning. The person we are most capable of deluding (conning, tricking, etc.) is our self. Whole industries exist based on this phenomenon (consider any of the "self-help" sections in your bookstore, try "dieting" as an example). The more you can adopt the attitude that you will only accept those descriptions of yourself that have been concretely established, the faster you will make progress. The classic example in archery is the indoor archer who has recently started shooting perfect 300 scores in 300 rounds. It is so easy when this happens to think of yourself as a "300 Shooter." But if you were to list all of your scores in that round, you would probably find that over 90% of your scores were not 300. You really shouldn't claim to be a 300 shooter until over 90% of your scores are 300 (minimum of your last 30 scores). This is a sound basis for the claim. If you label yourself incorrectly, you set up a state where your self-image says one thing and "you" are saying another. This is a prime cause of inconsistent performances.

Consequently practices need to be purpose-based and evaluated fairly, otherwise you are deluding yourself as to what you think you are accomplishing.

Bring Your Goals to You Imagine that you had a friend who wanted to become a world-class high jumper and asked for your help. You respond by noting that to be a world-class high jumper you have to be able to make a seven foot jump, so you suggest setting up a seven-foot bar and ask your friend to give it a try. He does and doesn't even come close to the bar, let alone clear it. So you say "Keep trying and let me know when you get there." This is a pretty stupid approach, no? This is a pretty stupid approach, yes. (But this is exactly how most archers approach practice.) You know what this high jumper should do, don't you? This is not rocket science. You start by finding out what height he can actually clear in a jump, and then you go to work on strength and flexibility training, as well as improving his technique. As progress is made, the bar is raised a little at a time until either the goal is met or he runs out of passion for the task. This is exactly how your archery practice needs to go and this is what the header of this paragraph means. Let me give you another example.

When I was working my way up the ladder in California field archery shooting a compound bow freestyle, I clawed my way up to making "A Class." And there I was at the bottom of "A Class" with no chance of winning anything. (There were a number of "competitors" who guaranteed they stayed at the top of "B Class" to ensure they won something, but I am sure you are not one of "those.") To make A Class at that time, you had to, in essence, average a score of 500 on a 560 point field round. Since there were 28 targets in that round, you had to average just under 18 points (out of 20) per target. This set up some easy scoring goals:

> For an average target score of . . . 18.0, the round score is 504.
> For an average target score of . . . 18.5, the round score is 518.
> For an average target score of . . . 19.0, the round score is 532.
> For an average target score of . . . 19.5, the round score is 551.

So, I set a goal of 518 and met it, then changed my goal to 532. Then I got derailed on this task, but that is another story. What I want to describe is what I was trying to do to reach the 532 score goal. In order to average 19 points per target, I had to shoot a lot of 19's and 20's, at least as many 20's as I shot scores of 18, and anything less than an 18 was a real setback. So, like many of you, I just shot practice round after practice round. Then I got another idea. I decided to shoot a round from the Cub's stakes. Yes, the Cub's stakes. Cubs are the NFAA Under 12 youth category and they shoot nothing over thirty yards. So, the 80 yard walk-up target with the biggest target the NFAA has . . . is shot from 30 yards. It should be impossible to miss, right? It was a real revelation. I sweated bullets shooting cleanly for fourteen targets. I had so many outside-in scores of 5, I stopped counting. I couldn't believe the pressure I felt. (And I was alone, no one was watching.) I just felt that missing would reveal some sort of flaw in me. I found out later that what I was experiencing was a conflict with my "self-image." In my mind, I was not one of the guys who shot in the 530's, 540's and 550's. I was a 530 wannabe. The further I got into that round, shooting clean (all 20's), the greater and greater pressure I felt. If I had missed, I probably would have felt relieved. (Actually I quit after the first 14 because I was afraid I would miss on one of the coming targets!)

What was happening to me, I found out later, is what happened to me during competition. I would shoot really well, and then make a mistake, knocking myself out of the competition and then I could relax. (I have discussed these phenomena—self image and comfort zones—in the previous chapter, if you haven't read it yet.)

To address this problem, it is necessary to convince yourself (your inner self) that you are capable of your goal, and just as in the case of the high jumper, you should not just keep trying to meet your goal by trying over and over. You need to bring the goal to you. What this means is instead of you slowly increasing your score until you reach success, go right to success (by lowering the bar) and then practice being successful as you slowly increase the difficulty of the task. Keep shooting the Cub's stakes until you are comfortable shooting all 20's. Then move to the Youth stakes (50 yards max) and repeat. Lower the bar and practice success. The "inner you" will get accustomed to shooting perfect or near perfect scores. Your "inner you" doesn't care that you are shooting at less than the standard distances, it just knows that you shoot twenties all of the time.

If you are working on the Vegas Round, start at 10 yards instead of the actual 20 yards, or even five yards. Use a larger than regulation target. Experience how it feels shooting lots of X's. Please don't think this is too easy. You have to try it and experience shooting 9's on your last arrow over and over again, to see how difficult it can be. (It is easy to lose focus because you think you shouldn't miss.) Slowly move the targets back, one or two yards at a time, and/or make the targets smaller until you are at the full distance with standard target.

If your goal is to shoot a 300 indoor score, move the target in, make the target larger until you can shoot 300 (over and over), then make the task incrementally harder and when you are done, you will be quite used to shooting spectacular scores. Also, you have built into this scheme an indicator of your progress.

Don't just keep trying to jump over a seven foot bar and practice failing!

Also, you need to keep your eyes and ears open to find practice regimens like this. The more you have, the better. If you are stuck with just one training regimen, it is easy to get bored. Switch to other drills as you need to stay fresh and focused on your challenge.

Having Said That . . .

While the above may be a little too "philosophical" for you there are a few simple principles that apply to all archery practice. Here is my list (in no particular order).

#1 *The form/execution element being worked on must be done more frequently than when just shooting.* Example If working on a new stance, don't just step up to the shooting line and empty your quiver. Step off the line after each shot and retake you stance. Example If your draw needs work, try "Double Draws." This involves drawing to take a shot, then letting down almost to brace (or to brace if a compound bow) and drawing again and then finishing the shot.

#2 *The only basis upon which a practice exercise/shot should be evaluated is the thing being worked on.* Example If you are working on having a soft, repeatable bow hand and you lose focus and put an arrow through an air conditioning duct but your bow hand was nice and soft, that was a "good shot."

This is why expert archers shoot without a target face (blank bale or even blind bale, that is with eyes closed) when working on form/execution elements. The target automatically supplies a judgment system that has nothing to do with what is being worked on.

#3 *Often when you change something significant, things get worse before they get better.* Generally this is a matter of focus. The new form/execution element attracts so much of your focus, you lose some on the other aspects of your shot.

The only true measure of whether a change is successful is whether your quality indicators (practice scores, group sizes, etc.) get better after getting worse when you make the change. There is an oft quoted adage that "it takes 21 days of practice to create a new habit." I have found no scientific evidence for this, but it serves as a reasonable guideline.

#4 *The most important aspect of archery to practice is relaxation.* To be successful, archers need to be able to relax and focus under the tension of the draw. Any muscles tensed that aren't needed to be tensed sap your energy, reduce your flexibility, and contribute to tension elsewhere in your body, including mental tension.

#5 *If you want your mental program to work in competition, it must be a regular part of your practice.* This sounds like an oxymoron but the vast majority of archers don't do it.

#6 *While you are shooting, if anything, anything at all—mental or physical—intrudes from your environment or from a prior step, you must let down and start over.* I call this the *Rule of Discipline.* If you willingly shoot shots that you know are not properly executed, you are giving your subconscious mind license to improvise on the fly. Instead you want your subconscious mind to monitor your shots and blow a whistle when you do something differently from what you practiced.

    This rule applies in practice; this rule applies in competition. The closer you adhere to this rule, the faster you will make progress.

#7 *Improvements are made in the order of one's shot sequence.* Because everything that comes later in a shot is dependent on what comes before, improvements are made from the start and then go to the finish. Example If your stance isn't right, fix it first. Everything else depends upon it. Work done on later steps prematurely will be wasted because when the stance is changed, everything following is changed, too.

#8 *The goal is to have all elements/phases of the shot at the same level of quality.* Just as a chain is only as strong as it's weakest link, an archery shot doesn't benefit from one or two strong elements as the weaker ones will determine the quality of the outcome. This is how one tells when to stop working on something: when a weak form element is brought up to the quality of the rest of the shot, move on to something else; continuing to work on something after that point will not make any overall improvement in your shot.

#9 *Once all elements (form and execution) are at the same level, shooting larger numbers of arrows to drill one's form home is warranted.* Anyone shooting large numbers of arrows before their shot is complete is only practicing "doing it wrong." As a rule of thumb, for every incorrect shot you take, you will need several correct shots to wash away the imprint of the poor shot. Shooting large numbers of arrows does not improve your shot, just your consistency (and your stamina). You do not want to be able to consistently shoot shots poorly.

#10 ***If one's shot has all of its pieces at the same level but performance is not good enough, the entire shot is rebuilt to a higher level, again following the shot sequence.*** Each step is modified to see if it can be improved. Some measure of "better" must be used.

#11 ***Only one thing can be worked on at a time.*** Because your conscious mind trains your subconscious mind and your conscious mind can only entertain one thought at a time, you must work on only one aspect of your shot at a time. If you change two things at the same time and things get better, was it because of Change A or Change B? Did both changes make you better or did Change A make you better and Change B make things worse? Or . . .

Now this doesn't mean you can't be working on multiple parts of your shot, it just means that you must focus on one, and only one, at a time.

Key Points
Chapter 7 Winning Practice

You will find a great deal about how to practice in most of the other chapters, but there were some things I just needed to say here that were unavoidable.

- Practice stands for so many things to archers that there is great confusion about what it is.
- If you don't know why you are practicing, specifically, you are probably wasting your time and quite probably deluding yourself.
- Never, ever practice doing something you know is wrong; fix it first.
- I do not believe that practicing for a set number of shots or for a set time can be right, let alone is right.
- A successful practice is one in which you accomplished what you were trying to accomplish.
- It is very easy to delude yourself which is why you need an outside point of view (from a coach or experienced shooting partner).
- Bring your goals to you by using larger targets at shorter distances and practice being successful by shooting high score after high score, working your way back to standard distances and standard size targets

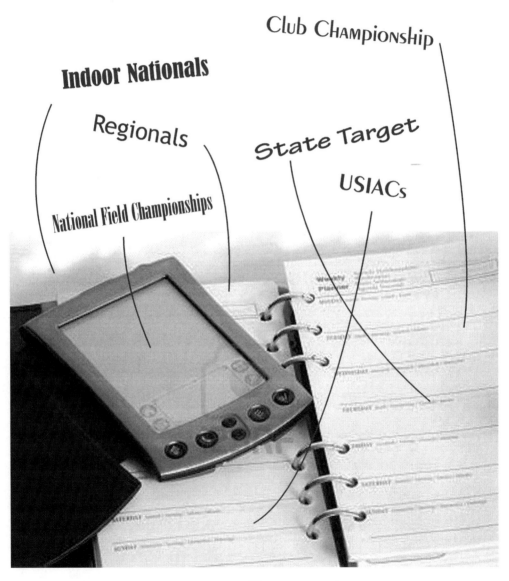

Club Championship

Indoor Nationals

Regionals

State Target

USIACs

National Field Championships

8

Planning to Win

So, you hear about this great little one-day tournament which draws people from all over the southern part of your state and you've decided to go and compete. From what you can learn, you are shooting very competitive scores for this event and have a high probability of winning. So, brimming with confidence, you drive to the event early in the morning, get set up and then go talk to the people at "Registration" to sign up. They ask for proof that you are a member of the sponsoring umbrella organization and you admit that you have not yet joined. You are told you may only shoot in "Guest" class and proceed to shoot a score almost 30 points higher than the person taking the gold medal in your competitive category.

How would you feel? (I can guess, because I have seen it happen quite a few times as a worker at registration tables at such events.)

The reason I tell this story is I do want you to feel the frustration of this: the dumbness, the stupidity, the arrrgh! Because all of these kinds of mistakes are avoidable with just a little planning. You will learn the lessons involved in learning how to compete—the question is: Do you want to learn these lessons the hard way or the easy way?

Can I Win?

Let us assume you have a goal of winning a particular tournament. Most recreational archers practice up and go to the tournament and try their best. If the very best archers are off of their games or don't show up, there is a reasonable chance of winning. If you want to have a good chance of winning, though, you can't depend on your competition being off or not showing up! You must assume they will be there and they will be "on." Assuming this is the case, what is your realistic chance of winning?

A good thing to know is what winning scores have been like in your competitive category. Once you know that, you then can ask yourself "Can I shoot such a score?" . . . at all, not just under the pressure of competition. If your practice scores are 20 points below what the winning scores have been for the last three years, you probably have no chance of winning—absolutely zero. So, let's look at this aspect of your preparation to win.

Planning to Win In order for you to win consistently, you must have reasonable expectations that winning is possible. If such reasonable expectations can't be made, you are just hoping to win. So, how do you go about creating these expectations?

Let's back up several months. You have made this goal (I will win Tournament X.) far enough in advance of the event that you can actually do something to enhance your chances. Making the goal when driving to the event only happens in the movies. Making the goal only a couple of weeks from the event really gives you no time to prepare. So, several months (or more) ahead of time you have made this goal. Now it is time to connect the dots. You are here now and in nine months you are on the winner's stand. How can you assure yourself you have a reasonable chance to win? Well, the first step involves knowing what the winning scores have been over the last few years. Then you must ask yourself "Can I shoot such a score?" You can't just answer this as "Sure I can!" brimming with confidence, you have to *prove* it. You must shoot such scores in practice, not just once in a while, but consistently. So, let's say you are close but not at the right level yet. Now you have to devise a plan whereby you will increase the level of your scoring to the new, higher (and needed to win) level. This is where a lot of people fail before they get started. They decide that what they need to do is shoot the competitive round over and over and surely their scores will go up. This is like taking an algebra test in school, failing it miserably, and deciding all you have to do is keep taking tests and you'll get better enough to score well. You wouldn't have done this in school, so why would you think it will work on archery scores? You know what you would have done to pass another algebra test, you would have studied more before taking another test, that is you would have practiced.

Well, isn't shooting practice rounds practice?

No! Shooting a practice round is a test of performance. This is not practice per se; this is a test to see how well practice is going. Shooting practice rounds bi-weekly, or more frequently if you are practicing daily, is absolutely essential, but if this is all you do, all you are doing is drilling your non-winning form. If you know the weak points in your form and execution, you must devise workouts that focus on bringing up those weak points until they are as strong as the rest of your shot. If you don't know what they are, you need help from a shooting partner or coach to help you identify them. Then you have to plan to do these things and then do them. Without the plan, you probably won't do what you need to do.

It Takes a ~~Village~~ Plan

Actually, in the next chapter I will address the "it takes a village" aspect of becoming and staying a winning archer, but right now we need to address the planning required. And there is quite a bit going on that can separate you from the winning circle.

A major point is that with just a little planning you can avoid making mistakes that can cost you championships while you are learning all of what is needed.

Things like not bringing enough arrows to an event or not having kept your dues paid up in an archery organization whose membership is required to compete for medals.

A key point here is you will save yourself a lot of grief if you will just write a few things down. Another key point is you only have so much focus to expend and if you waste it on dealing with lost luggage or getting lost in a strange town, you aren't going to have enough focus left to be competitive.

You will hear a lot of people say "experience is the best teacher;" what you don't hear them say is "it is the best teacher because it is brutal, heartless, and cruel." Why not learn from other people's experience and minimize the pain?

Basic Planning You do not need a college degree in event planning to manage a "career" as a winning archer, but you do need a few plans. At a minimum you need at least three plans: a practice plan (parts of this are dynamic and change from week to week), a training plan, and a competition plan. You may want to include other plans, if you decide to do fundraising, for example.

These plans don't have to be written out, but I will warn you now, if you don't write things down, the number of things you miss or forget or mistake will be larger than if you do. You don't have to be the plan designer or even the plan writer. Someone else can do it for you, but if you do not support the planning process, it will not be effective.

"Do I really need to do these things?" you ask.

Not a good question. The answer: Yes!

There are so many distractions that top archers face, it is easy to get off track. I had a conversation with Dave Cousins, who had been at the top of FITA compound archer world rankings, and I was asking him about doing a magazine article on the seminars he was giving. The seminars were quite popular and proved profitable for him, but he told me he had put all of those seminars on the shelf for a year, because while he was doing them, he wasn't focused on his own practice and, worse, he was focused on other people's problems, and it had affected his performance negatively. Wow, it seemed a great idea: a workshop from a world champion archer, available at your local archery shop, affordable, too. And such workshops are very valuable, but there is a cost to the presenter. This is why you don't find people with healthy competitive careers also doing much coaching, doing seminars, etc. Staying competitive takes quite a bit of effort and then there is work or school and family and so forth.

So, even top archers can be distracted from their main mission. (I just noticed that Dave is back on top as the FITA World Field Archery Champion.)

If you have a plan, you can look at your plan and list out how much time it takes to execute your plan and then see if you can fit another activity in. If not, you have to identify what it is you are going to leave out. This is what plans provide: a structure to help you make good decisions.

If you think, "Well, I am never going to put on seminars, that doesn't apply to me," think again.

It is not just seminars. I have talked to hundreds of archers about meeting one of their goals: getting sponsored. Getting sponsored can mean lower equipment costs, appearance money, travel money, winner's stipends, etc. Win a major competition and you may end up getting checks from many of the equipment companies whose equipment you shoot. But a lot of people don't think it through. When you sign a sponsorship agreement you are agreeing for your name and likeness to appear in that company's advertising. Which means you are agreeing to being photographed. They also may want you to do small seminars or appear in their booth at a trade show, or . . . or. . . . Sponsorships are not just icing on your archery cake, they come with obligations. And if you are a champion archer, you may just get offered sponsorships. Are you going to turn down free bows? Free arrows? Money? Probably not. So, you need to ask a lot of questions about what you will be required to do as part of these agreements. And you need to incorporate those activities in your plans.

Planning Data

Since there are likely to be several important tournaments you are focused on, you will probably have several plans within your plan. Often, competing at a tournament is a means to an end rather than an end in itself. If you are primarily a target archer competing on a flat field but you have a goal of competing well at a particular field archery tournament (to make a national team and get a free trip overseas!), it is in your best interest to schedule several field tournaments prior to the main event. You may need to knock the rust off of your field archery skills (shooting up-, down-, and side-hill shots, for example, or just reacquainting yourself with having to carry everything you might need with you).

Practice Scores vs. Competition Scores A really important piece of information is how your practice scores compare to your competition scores. There are two common patterns. One type of archer thrives on competition. This archer is energized and focused by the event. His scores at competitions are higher than his practice scores. The other type of archer tenses up and generally performs worse in competition than she does in practice. The question is: what does this information tell you?

First, if your competition scores tend to be 5-10% higher than practice scores, then your practice scores only need to be close to the level of a winning score for you to be ready to compete and win. If your practice scores are higher than your competition scores, you must get your practice scores even higher to account for that. There are implications for the way you practice also.

If You are a Competition Animal You outshoot your practice scores in competition. In competition, you never seem to get tired. You are animated, focused. You thrive. What do you need in practice? You need better practice scores. If you raise your practice scores, your competition scores will rise with them. Often this kind of archer doesn't fully focus during practice sessions; it is, after all, just practice. Helping you learn to focus includes such things as:

1. *Be more demanding of yourself.* Often outsiders aren't as demanding of "star" athletes as we could be, so if you are very competitive and win a lot, you may think subconsciously that you don't "need" much practice. If your coach isn't that demanding or doesn't seem to become more demanding if you ask him/her to be, maybe you need another coach. If you are working on your own, add stuff to your practice plans. Don't stop practice early. Make a personal commitment to work hard.

2. *Set up practice sessions to be more like competitions.* Have shootoffs between you and your shooting partner or invite other archers for a little friendly competition practice. Handicap these competitions to put more scoring pressure on yourself, e.g. add distance or use a smaller target or spot your opponent points, to make sure you work hard. Have a prize for winning the contest—a soda is too easy, maybe one will wash the other's car, something you'd rather not to have to pay off.

If You are a Practice Animal You shine in practice but labor in competition. This is a more complicated situation. The root causes can be anything from your coach being the one you truly want to please, to performance anxiety, to a self image issue.

1. If the issue is performance anxiety, raising practice scores helps. If competition scores are 8-10% below practice scores, would you rather have 90-92% of 1150 or 1220? The techniques to raise practice scores are as described above (amongst many others).

2. If the issue is a self image issue there are good exercises to change your self-image. For one, see "Getting There v. Being There" above. This exercise can even work for Competition Animals in that it is easy to lose focus and miss. Don't be surprised if you get frustrated and tell everyone nearby that you think the exercise is stupid! This just tells you it is working; in fact, it is so easy, anyone could do it.

The goal is for your practice scores to be very nearly the same as your competition scores. This tells you that your scoring is dependable. This tells you that your focus in practice and competition is consistent. This tells you that you have constructed a practice environment that is as difficult as competition. This means that your practice experience will lap over into being competition experience and not be discounted as being "just practice" any more. To do this you need to . . . make scoring in practice like scoring in competition.

Making Practice Like Competition You will be at a disadvantage if you have never shot at the venue of the competition. Outdoors, the angle of the sun, the wind, the terrain (if field archery), and many other factors can affect your performance. Indoors, there is a different set of factors, the primary one being lighting. I have shot indoors in armories where if you are at the end of the line, you were shooting virtually in the dark and if you were in the center, the lighting was fine. If your indoor practice site has darkly colored bales, will you be affected by the fact that at the Vegas Shoot the bales are white? Absolutely! There are a number things you can do to offset this experience factor. For one, you can attend a competition without the goal of winning, just to get that experience. You will have goals for the competition and you may end up winning the thing, but the goal is to experience the venue and the flow of the competition. You can get photographs from friends or off of the Internet, that will tell you something about the lighting and orientation of the range. You can collect information from friends and fellow competitors about the quirks of the venue. (Don't get anywhere near the kitchen, man, they are always dropping pots and pans!)

If your target will be up against a white background and your practice range has dark bales, you can pin a white sheet up to pin your target face to for your practice rounds to see if this has any effect on your sight settings or your practice scores. If the venue is noisy, turn on a radio and crank it up. Make sure it is set to a station which plays something obnoxious: music you don't like, Rush Limbaugh, something else really irritating. And, of course, you must follow all of the tournament rules. If you have to move your target face mid-way in a round, do it. If you must shoot on a clock, do it. If you can arrange for your training partner to shoot against you in the next lane, do it.

You must, repeat must, be aware of all of the rules associated with the shoot. I am not encouraging you to become a sports lawyer and protest every little accommodation made by the tournament organizers, but it is imperative that you know your rights under the rules. If you neglect to shoot an arrow, are you allowed a makeup arrow and when? Can you protest a judge's call? What is the procedure? Are there decisions a judge cannot make? What do you do about an arrow call you think is wrong? How many minutes and how many practice shots are you allowed for an equipment malfunction? You need to know the answers to these questions, if for no other reason than to keep your mind free from confusion. It will also help you when someone on your target tries to cheat. It doesn't happen often, but if you stay in the game long enough. . . .

Practice Planning

This whole book focuses on what you need to know and do other than "shoot well," and probably the biggest thing keeping people from shooting well and shooting well consistently is the fact that they have no idea what a practice should consist of. So, guys go to a practice range and tinker with their equipment, shoot a bunch of arrows, sight in, or maybe shoot a practice round. And at the next practice, they do much the same. Ask them what their "practice regimen" or "practice plan" is and the most thoughtful will say "I try to make practice as much like competition as I can." Sound familiar? The question is, though, do they? Let's look at this.

Practice Throughout the Year

In late summer, the outdoor season is winding down, typically after the last major championships of the outdoor season. It is at this point, while you are still shooting outdoors, you should get your indoor bow out of storage and review any notes you made last spring about changes you may have wanted to make. If you want to change, say, your arrow rest to a new style, you should schedule testing of the new rest against the old rest for early on. You should check all of your recorded measurements to make sure nothing has changed while the bow was put away. If you are setting up new arrows, you need to cut the shafts, fletch them, and add points, weight matching them as much as is needed. Then schedule your earliest practices to group shoot these arrows to make sure you create sets of them that group well at the distances being shot. Some of this you can do as the outdoor season is running down, as mainly it provides a nice distraction from what can be monotonous shooting practice.

In the 4-6 weeks before the indoor season really gets underway, check your notes to see if there are any form or execution changes you want to make and schedule practices to work on those during this period. You want everything—"equipment-wise" and "form and execution-wise"—to be settled by the time competitions begin. Schedule some casual competitions or league indoor shoots to test your rig and form before the important shoots come along.

Toward the end of indoor season, roughly mid-Spring, do the same things for your outdoor equipment to get ready for the outdoor season.

I never make equipment or form changes at the end of a season. I make notes! (I learned this the hard way. Make changes in your equipment at the end of a season and when something goes wrong with it when you pull it out of storage, you have no stored "feel" to use to help you figure out what went wrong. So, the first part of making an equipment change is to set up and shoot your rig in the "old" configuration and establish some benchmarks (scores, X-counts, etc.) and then make the change and test it (significantly!).

All of these things including individual practice plans belong as part of your annual practice plan.

Now let's look at each of these Practice Activities in more detail.

The Three Parts of Practice

There are three broad categories of practice activities and a framework that ties them together. When the activities are to be done is based on a framework. Here's the scheme:

The Framework The framework for your plans is the "archery year" broken into "archery seasons," roughly from mid-Spring to mid-Fall is "Outdoor Season," and from mid-Fall to mid-Spring is "Indoor Season." These are just rough, but you won't find too many indoor events overlapping with outdoor events and vice-versa. Exactly when the changeover between the two seasons is is determined mostly by your local climate. There are several weeks between seasons in which very few competitions are taking place.

Practice Category #1 This is what most people do (trying to make practice as much like competition as possible). This is done during the indoor and outdoor seasons, but not between seasons.

Practice Category #2 This includes shooting drills to correct and enhance technique, practicing shooting under unfamiliar conditions (slope, wind, etc.). These are typically done between seasons, but not during seasons.

Practice Category #3 This category includes all of the bow/arrow setup, tuning, equipment refinements, etc. These are typically done between seasons, but not during seasons.

Your plans need to take into consideration all of these activities in their own "seasons" as it were. Let me give you an idea of what a typical year might look like.

Practice Category #1 Activities

Again, this is what most people mean when they use the word "practice," namely practice rounds, simulated competitions, shooting rounds blank bale, friendly competitions with buddies, etc. Here are some ideas to include in your practice and, I hope, to enliven them. The key element in practice is focus—without it there is no dedicated practice and learning and progress will be slow. Anything that increases focus is all to the good.

Field Course Tips I came up as a field archer and I did all the wrong things (just to test them out, of course). Most aspiring archers do everything they can to increase their practice scores (a good idea) but they do it the wrong way. Most shoot their own range, their favorite targets (I always shot NFAA Hunter targets better than the field targets for some reason.), they shoot at a favorable time of day, in favorable weather, etc. On the contrary, you want to make it more difficult, not less. Start at a different target each time, shoot targets in different order, shoot every other target (1, 3, 5, 7, 11, 13, 2, 4, 6, 8, 10, 12, 14), shoot different lanes indoors when shooting practice rounds, set goals for X-ring count.

Make it harder not easier (like wannabes and newly arrived competitors do, wanting to brag about practice round scores). Track your scores and impact points (see the sidebar "Logging Your Practice Scores") and keep a journal for your practice sessions (conditions, mental states, attitudes, scores, X counts, inside-out X counts, etc.)

Target Range Tips Move around on the field, don't just camp out under your favorite tree. Practice shooting from sun into shade and shade into sun. Don't pack up and go when the wind kicks up or it starts to rain. While I don't recommend a lot of rain and wind practice, some is actually necessary. You need to try shooting in your rain gear, learn how to shoot with a wet tab, or when your 'scope gets wet. Test out your system for allowing for the wind drift of arrows. You want to know how your practice round scores are affected.

Indoor Range Tips Shoot different lanes indoors when shooting practice rounds, set goals for X-ring or 10-ring counts. Shoot patterns on multi-spot targets and vary the pattern from session to session, you may find one better than the one you thought "best." Try to shoot at as many different ranges as you can; different backgrounds and different lighting can affect sight settings significantly.

These are activities typically done during a competitive season: more intensively toward the beginning and less intensely when more and more competitions are being shot.

Practice Category #2 Activities

Some of these creep into most people's practices, but far too little is being done. There are a great many shooting drills that can be done (even at home and without a bow) that can improve your form and execution.

Field Course Tips If you have been struggling with up-, down-, or side-hill shots, practice these for a whole day. As long as it is allowed by your range, arrange such shots even if you must shoot from somewhere other than the normal shooting stakes. If you have no side-hill shots on your range, take a piece of plywood big enough to stand on and nail a 2x4 to one edge. You can now slant your shooting position from right to left or left to right. Contrary to what some people say, a hill exerts no significant gravitational pull on your arrows and is not needed for practice. The "side-hill effect" comes from the feeling that you "might fall downhill," so you don't stand straight up and down (you tend to lean into the hill).

If you shoot with a 'scope,' practice "bubbling" (¼, ½, 1 bubble left and right) and see how far the arrow impact points move to the left and right at various distances. I once shot every target on my home range with my sight set five yards high and five yards low to see how high and low the arrows would hit. (I marked the impact points on a printout I made of dummy target faces and I was surprised at how consistently high and low the impact points were, probably from the target faces being sized larger for longer distances, etc. I now have a good idea how much "off" I am when I miss high or low.)

Once when I was addressing a case of target panic, I went around my field range and went to every shooting position and drew on the target and settled in before making a let down and requivering the arrow. I didn't shoot an arrow for the hour or so that took. If, for no other reason, I found it much easier to let down after that exercise and it did help my target panic.

I have gone around a field range shooting the Cub Stakes. For one, I didn't get to shoot those stakes as a youth and another, I thought it would really be embarrassing to miss (the 80 yard target from 30 yards, for example). More than a couple of shots were "outside-in" spots and toward the end of the round I was sweating bullets trying to keep the round "perfect."

Target Range Tips Try shooting larger targets up close and really learn how to aim. Rick McKinney claims that, in a FITA Round and for Olympic-style men, the 90 meter and 50 meter distances are shot more from a base of rhythm, while the 70 meter and 30 meter distances are shot more by aiming hard. The aiming distances are the ones to work on with the bigger targets at the shorter distances. Of course, if you shoot a compound bow freestyle, it is always an aiming distance and this is good practice.

Shoot the big target up close and score a 30 arrow round, move it back five yards and score another round, another five yards and another round. (You can do this with an 80cm target face rather than the 122cm face, but psychologically, using the larger target face and hitting the gold that much is good for your self esteem.) Look at your scores. They should drop consistently as the target moves back. But what if they do not, what if they drop drastically at one point or, in fact, go up? What does that tell you?

If the wind starts blowing, practice your wind shooting! If not, prepare for it. You can practice aiming off by deliberately mis-setting your sight's windage adjustment then figure out where you have to aim to get the arrows to land in the gold. How is your score affected when "aiming off?" What about your group size? Practice aiming off both left and right and then add mis-setting the sight for the distance, too, so that you will need to aim high and left, and low and right, etc. If you shoot with a 'scope,' practice bubbling (¼, ½, 1 bubble left and right) and see how far the arrow impact points move to the left and right at various distances. Compare how effective bubbling is versus aiming off using group size as the criterion as to which you do better.

When you do practice wind shooting, pay attention to your rhythm. No one keeps the exact same rhythm they have in still air, but what happens to yours? Many people "ride the wind" by paying close attention to when they draw. If you draw right when the wind is at a peak, often it will fall off shortly thereafter and you will be at full draw and releasing when the wind is lower. Can you do this? How does it feel? You are not so much trying to discover "your wind rhythm" because the wind is not exactly consistent, but you are practicing how to find a rhythm that will work when the wind blows.

Indoor Range Tips Indoors is a wonderful place to practice certain skills as there is no variation in wind, rain, humidity, angle of the sun, terrain, etc. Indoor drills focus on aiming and execution. Whether you are a recurve or compound shooter, there are many games that can be played. Typically, start up close, even using a bigger target and shoot a very high (better, perfect) score. Get used to hitting the gold/spot. If you are a compound archer and you want to shoot perfect scores, should you stand back at the full distance and fire away, hoping one day you get there? People have done it, but that is definitely the hard way. Start with a bigger target, up close, and shoot perfect scores, shoot inside-out X's! When you get bored with perfect scores, move the target back 2-3 yards/meters and repeat. When you get bored shooting perfect scores, move the target back or switch to a smaller target. All of the gold/spot shooting done reinforces your subconscious mind with the idea that you "always hit the gold/spot" which is all to the good.

Variations on this involve a multi-spot target. Up close shoot five ends of five arrows or ten ends of three arrows if a three-spot target is used. If you shoot a perfect score, move the target back two yards and repeat. If you miss the 10-ring/spot, you move closer to the target two yards and repeat. Some like to make this drill brutal and send themselves all of the way back to where they began when they miss! You can make up your own rules for these games/drills.

Shooting blank and blind bale are techniques for finding the "feel" of your shot.

Combine shooting three arrow ends of blank bale with shooting ends of two arrows blank bale and the third arrow at a target, trying to preserve all of the feel you experience shooting without the target. Alternate with shooting one arrow blank bale and two at a target, again trying to preserve the feel of the shot.

There are a great many drills floating around, try to identify ones you think can help your game. (I have a project to collect as many drills as I can find all in one place for your reference, but that is not ready just yet. I will publish it in *Archery Focus* magazine when it is done.)

These activities are typically done before a competitive season: less intensively toward the beginning and more intensely just before competitions begin being contested. They can also be used for in-season "fixes," that is you have picked up a bad habit along the way and you need some intense work to correct it. For example, I picked up the problem of "dropping my bow arm," and later I discovered there is a drill for that. All you do is shoot blank bale after taking your bow sight off of your bow, sighting off of a knuckle of your bow hand. The objective is to keep that knuckle lined up with what ever reference in the butt you used through the shot (to do so, of course, you cannot drop your bow arm). This must be repeated a great deal to "break the bad habit."

Practice Category #3 Activities

Too many archers approach their equipment in "tinkering mode." Changes are made and almost instant judgments are made as to whether things are good or bad. This is the equivalent to thinking the "brightness" control of your TV will increase the sophistication of the programs viewed on it. If you want to avoid problems, I strongly recommend that you be very systematic about your equipment. Document every change by measuring the "before" and "after" status of your equipment. Have a test set up to help you decide whether making that particular change actually did any good. And always, always, make only one change at a time.

This is coming from a guy who started out putting a compound bow in a bow press, stripping the bowstring and cables off, putting new ones on, and taking the rig to the range to see "how it shoots now." Boy, how dumb can you get? Now, I make my own bowstrings and cables and changing a set takes a considerable amount of time and effort. But when I am done, the draw length and brace height are the same as when I began.

When you decide to set up new arrows, what is your procedure? For me, if they are replacements, I know how long to cut them and what point weight I need and what vanes to use. So, it is a simple assembly job . . . well, I do weigh all of the components, eliminate any odd parts, and weight match the arrows as much as is desirable. I then label each arrow and shoot test them. Some archers will shoot test them before fletching them! I prefer to have more than one dozen arrows available but I don't always have the budget for that. If I do have the budget for more than one dozen, my goal is to get a couple of competitive sets from the bundle. I may have a half dozen arrows that group really well but at shorter distances and another half dozen that group best at longer distances. What would you do if you found this was the case? Use the better grouping long distance arrows for longer distance shoots, maybe? The point is you can't do this if you don't have the information.

To group test your arrows you need to number them temporarily and then shoot them at various distances. I just print out target facsimiles and write the arrow numbers on the impact points. If arrow #3 consistently hits low and left, I might try replacing and/or rotating the nock of that arrow. If arrow #5 hits first here then there, then over there, I may rebuild it (nock replacement first), or just consign it to being a blank bale practice arrow.

If you have sets with different characteristics, you can number the sets: Set A— A-1, A-2, A-3, etc. and Set B—B-1, B-2, B-3, etc.

This is not new stuff, longbow archers of 80 years ago "clocked" their arrows, e.g. an arrow labeled with a "6" tended to land toward 6 o'clock on the target so aim a little higher, etc. Arrows are more regular now, but they are not perfect.

If you want to compare one particular new arrow against your old arrows, have a contest. Shoot a practice round of ten ends: in the odd ends shoot your old arrows, in the even ends shoot the new ones. (You will probably have different sight settings so you will have to adjust for each end.) Do this for three or four practice sessions. Which arrows provided the better score? Which ones should you shoot? This is not a perfect process, either, because if you tweak one set of the arrows it might shoot substantially better. I have known archers who switched arrow sponsors and then the next year switched back to their old sponsor. Guess why? Sometimes it can take a year to figure it out.

So, you really like your new tab! Will you like it as well when it starts to rain? Get out a spray bottle and douse it down and test it. Do your scores hold up? Is the wet tab slippery? Does the wet tab make you nervous?

You got some really cool new rain gear . . . are you going to wait for a tournament to try it out? Not if you want to win consistently.

The Practice Plan

So, what has to be in your practice plan?

All of the above.

You need to set aside pages (yes, you are going to write it down, otherwise you will forget or miss something) for daily practice plans and you need a plan (it may just be a list of 2-3 things you are going to do) for each practice session. You need to set aside room for notes: notes about your equipment, your form, your execution, etc.

Having all of this together (with all of your other plans) is a good idea as stuff that comes up after a tournament can be things you want to address in a subsequent practice session.

A multi-section spiral bound notebook is inexpensive and already broken into parts for you—makes a good "planner."

A really important aspect of planning is the impact of goals. As I mentioned in the chapter on assessing where you stand, if you want to win a tournament, you have to be capable of shooting a winning score. A little research will tell you what winning scores have been for the past few years. Let's say you need to shoot a field round score of 535 to win, but your best round so far has been a 522. To bridge that gap, you are much better off establishing the goal to shoot a 525 and after you have done that, shoot a 530, and after that a 535, than you are just setting a goal of 535 for your practice round scores. Think about it. If you just set the 535 goal and fail time after time to meet it and you end up leaving for the tournament with the thought "maybe I'll get lucky," how well do you think that will work? But if you try and try and finally meet the 525 goal (and celebrate it) and then try and try to meet the 530 goal and then meet it (and celebrate it), even if you don't meet the 535 goal, don't you think you will be more confident that if you just failed time after time to meet the big goal? And, if you did meet the 535 score goal for a practice round, how about the goal of averaging 535 in your practice rounds, how about 540? If you have met every goal you have set yourself, you have to believe you can meet these goals to.

Outcome goals can be a very powerful tool when used correctly, that is to build "ladders of success." Write your goals down, review them before every practice round. Set goals for X-ring counts, etc. All of these make for more focus which pays off in better practice and better performance. My all-time best field practice round occurred when I set myself the goal to have no single target score less than 18/20. (On the 80-yard walk up, I had a mental lapse and started by shooting a three. The next three arrows had considerable focus attached to them and I came away with an 18.) And I know archers who think an 18 is a disgrace. Everyone's goals should start where they are and work up toward where they want to be. A series of successes builds a lot more confidence that a lofty goal never met.

Training Planning
This is where you put all of your training plans. Include both physical training (strength and cardio conditioning plans, etc.) and mental training plans. These do not have to be extensive but if you are serious about these activities, you will need to do them regularly, plus you need goals and need to log your activities (physical training involves exercise sets, numbers of repetitions, etc.). If you schedule practicing new mental skills, you are more likely to incorporate them into ordinary practices which is the only way they become useful (by becoming habitual). Don't try a bunch of things at once. Pick a mental tool. Pick a time to practice it. Pick a date you will incorporate using it in your ordinary practice sessions, pick a date when you will do an evaluation of whether you fee that tool was effective at all and, if so, under what circumstances.

Competition Planning
Have you ever overheard the conversation, "Are you going to <Indoor Nationals or whatever>?"

"I dunno, are you going?"

"Yeah!"

"Cool, maybe I'll go, too."

Heck, I have not only overheard such conversations, I have taken part in them. Such is the life of a recreational archer. But if you want to be a successful competitive archer, you need to be a little more deliberate.

Well before a competitive season, pick the tournaments that will highlight the season for you: national, sectional, international, the biggies. These you really want to go to. If attending these means making a national team or shooting a qualifying score, you then need to attend to those tasks. What is needed to make the national team? What competitions need you attend and what placements or scores do you need at those? If you think your chances are poor of achieving those teams or scores, it changes a great deal of what you might be doing compared with if you think your chances are very, very good. You work your way back from these high import events to events of less and less importance, but which build your standing or prepare you for the more intense competition to come. Build "success ladders" from the less important events to the more important events.

Attending just your own club's events and then heading to nationals is not a recipe for success. You want to be shooting at a variety of ranges, under a variety of conditions. If the key event is shot at high altitude or in a windy location, you are going to want to take on a few warm up events that involve high elevation and/or wind, that sort of thing.

If the big shoots are multi-day events, you don't want to limit yourself to single day preparatory events. If the field course of the big event is quite hilly and your home range is flat, get out of town for a while!

This is not rocket science. In fact, most people tend to go to the same events year after year. They develop a competitive circuit of their own, but do realize you do need to mix things up if the conditions of the big shoot change dramatically from last year.

You need an outdoor plan and an indoor plan and you need them before the season starts. Do realize that you can change things up. You can add, remove, or switch events around. But if you have thought about all of the factors involved when you first made up the plan, it will be easier to make good decisions when you look at how such changes fit in with the other things you have scheduled.

Also part of competition planning is travel planning, especially if you are going to foreign counties. If there is jet lag involved, you do not want to be flying in the morning of a competition. Also, just sitting for hours in an airplane or a car can be debilitating for an athletic performance. I also recommend you inquire as to the food available. If the cuisine of that region or country is not agreeable, you are going to want to research where you can eat agreeable food. You may have to go to grocery stores and buy ingredients to cook yourself. You may want to arrange for a motel room with a kitchenette to be able to cook for yourself. If you travel with others, you need to plan along with them.

Is your passport up to date?

Miscellaneous Planning

Anything you are going to do that requires more than a little effort is worth planning. If you are going to undertake international competitions, you will quickly learn that the bulk of it is "self funded." Yes, if you make certain national teams, you get supported travel (you will still have some out-of-pocket expenses) but few archers get these gigs and often it is the same people from year to year as archery is a sport where one can compete at a high level for many years.

So, if you are "well to do" as my parents used to say, you can afford these trips, but for the rest of us raising travel funds is a necessity. You will have to be involved in this, no matter how good your support team is, so getting the activities scheduled and organized requires that plans be made.

You may find yourself doing school demonstrations, public speaking, appearances at trade shows for sponsors, etc. You can either have these happen to you or you can make them positive experiences with a little planning. Think about it.

Tying It All Together

Computers make things so much easier. In the "old days" one would take a paper calendar and start writing in things. With "Calendar Creator" or even Google *Calendar*, you can set up an archery-specific calendar with all of your activities logged in: physical training routine days, mental training activities, coaching sessions formal practices, competitions, etc. You can have all of your organization all in one place and you can even access these things on a smart phone or PDA. Well worth doing.

Sidebar—Logging Your Practice Scores

You may be aware that professional golfers keep way more statistics than just their scores: number of fairways hit, number of greens in regulation, numbers of putts, sand saves, etc. Heck, if you are on the PGA Tour they keep all of these statistics for you and you can log onto their website and get very detailed information about the length of your drives, how close to the pin are your approach shots (on average), how you do on Par 3, 4, and 5 holes on average, how many feet of putts you make, as well as comparisons with the statistics of all of the other Tour players.

Archers don't get such service, but we can provide it to ourselves, actually quite simply. For example, in your practice rounds, you should use an individual arrow scoring card (if you can't buy them, just make one—it's just a table you can make in a word processor, like Microsoft *Word*). When you score the arrows, I often scoring them in the order they are shot and not the way they are scored in competition (highest scoring to lowest). This is easier on multi-spot targets. Also, each arrow can even be scored to the tenths place!

For example, an arrow just missing the 5-ring would be scored a 4.9. Half way out in the four ring is a 4.5 and just barely into the five is a 5.1 (a "jar licker" 5 is a 5.0, a dead center X is a 5.5). This tells me if my misses are "just out" or "way out." I also write a little number in the upper right hand corner "11" if the arrow was at the 11 o'clock position, 6 if straight low in the 6 o'clock position. Other people feel this is too slow and they just put a dot or a check mark in the upper left hand corner for "high, left" arrows, a dot in the lower right-hand corner for "low, right" hits, etc.

Some quick and dirty analysis can be had by just adding up the hits in each of those four quadrants. The patterns exposed can expose some form flaws.

If you record your arrows in the order shot, especially on multi-spot targets, you can see if you have patterns based on the order of shooting. If your final shots are generally weak, it may be a sign that you are shooting too quickly (not enough recovery time between shots) or maybe your fitness needs to be attended to. If your initial shots score poorly, there are mental routines to assist with that. If you discover such a pattern, you definitely want to examine the results of shooting that multi-spot target in a different sequence. You may want to explore shooting the spots in different orders, if so, put it in your practice plan.

You can also make up facsimile targets in a computer drawing program and print them out. Write the arrow number at each point an arrow hits. From this you can determine your score, whether your "misses" were close or not, and whether you have any problem target spots or problem arrows.

An option not available a while ago, is you can just start with a fresh target before your scoring round, and take a photo of the target with a camera (or cell phone) and email it to your computer. From just this little trick, you can examine the pattern of hit points with your known shooting sequence and see if you have any problems.

And, if you have the resources, there are software programs that allow you to log your shots on simulated targets and then give you substantial feedback on your rounds. These work on PDAs and tablets, and even smart phones.

Key Points
Chapter 8 Planning to Win

Most people don't want to do this. Heck, I don't want to do this, but someone on your team needs to.

- You will learn the lessons involved in learning how to compete—the question is do you want to learn these lessons the hard way or the easy way?
- Shooting practice rounds isn't practice, shooting practice rounds is a test of performance.

- If shooting practice rounds is all you do, all you are doing is drilling your non-winning form.
- You only have so much focus to expend and if you waste it on dealing with lost luggage or getting lost in a strange city, you aren't going to have enough left to be competitive.
- Expectations of winning must be based on facts (practice scores compared with competition scores, etc.) not just on hopes.
- Making practice more like competition can make you more consistent and reliable.
- Plan your activities by season (indoor and outdoor) and by looking months ahead of time.
- The key element in practice is focus—without it there is no dedicated practice . . . and learning and progress will be slow. Anything that increases focus is all to the good.
- It is better to make practice harder rather than easier by breaking up routines and shooting in different lanes, target sequences, etc.
- Practice aiming off and shooting from poor footing and other skills by artificially creating such scenarios.
- Indoors is a wonderful place to practice certain skills as there is no variation in wind, rain, humidity, angle of the sun, terrain, etc. so that you can really focus on aiming and execution.
- Between seasons is a great time to do drills that improve your form, execution, and self image.
- Part of practice time is taken up with equipment investigations; be very systematic about these efforts, otherwise much of your practice time can be wasted.
- Your practice plan has to have plans for daily practices, equipment tests, drills you want to do, your goals, everything—plus room for you to make notes.
- Your training plan has to include your strength and cardio conditioning plans and your mental training plans.
- Your competition plan has to include those events you are focused on and "success ladders" you use to reach the goals you have for those events. You also need to include travel planning for events far enough away that you must stay overnight.
- Making up a master calendar or set of calendars (easy to do now on a computer) will provide you an easy structure for all of your plans.
- There are many ways to "mine" useful data from your practice rounds. Don't miss out by just recording your end scores.

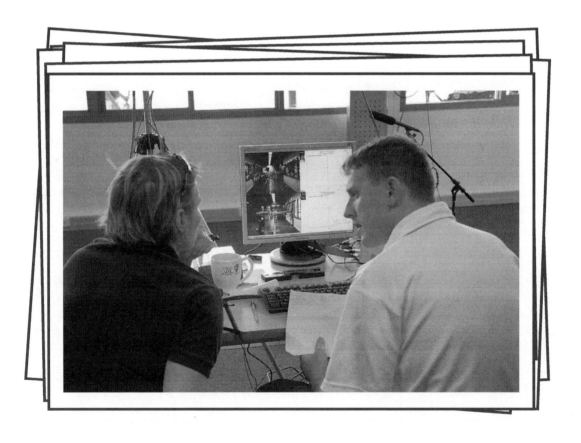

9

Developing Your Support Team

There are a few "lone wolf" archers who handle everything themselves, but they are a rarity. In general, behind every successful archer, there is a support team. This is especially true if you are a young archer. People will come and go in your support team, but primarily it includes: your parents or spouse, your coach, and secondarily: relatives, siblings, practice partners, competitors, officials, physical trainers, sports psychologists, and more.

At a bare minimum your support team is fueled by your appreciation of what they do for you, so you must pay attention and notice what is being done . . . and appreciate it. Do your parents drive you to events, pay for your equipment, pay your coach, take vacation time from work, etc. to support your participation as a competitive archer? Does you spouse go with you to weekend events, even when he/she is a nonarcher? Much of what spouses give up can be somewhat invisible. They are giving up time with you! Time that would be spent on home improvement projects, recreational activities, etc. If you have children, they are foregoing time spent with you, so that you can pursue your practice.

This must be appreciated and, in some form or other, must be returned at some point. If you build up a big time debt pursuing winning archery, time with spouse and/or family must be repaid in some fashion. If not, you can be undermining your own family.

Yes, I am very serious. If you seriously pursuing winning archery, many of those closest to you have to sacrifice something significant to support you. If you take their support for granted, you may lose them and their support later.

This is called "pay back." Start thinking about it now: "How can I pay back those who are supporting me?" If M. Scott Peck is right and "Love is time," you will need to go way out of your way to make sure you have some non-archery-related time to spend with members of your team as part of your appreciation of what they do for you.

If you are young, appreciation comes in the form of helping out around the house when asked and all of the other things "good kids" do. It means understanding when the family budget just doesn't have enough leeway to get you a new pair of limbs or a new bow. Your loved ones don't expect you to pay them for their time or provide gas money to offset their travel expenses nor do they expect you to get a job and pay them back for the archery equipment they supply. But appreciation is not hard to provide; it starts with simple "thank yous."

While you may end up depending on sisters and brothers, practice partners, archery club officers and any number of other folks, the key "players" on your support team are your parents or spouse and your coach. I have addressed parents and spouses above with the simple message that there needs to be appreciation and pay back. In more detail below we will be looking at coaches: finding them, keeping them, dumping them, etc.

Get a Coach

It is a fact that the vast majority of people who identify themselves as "archers" in this country have probably never been coached. They were, as I was, taught by friends. Archers are social animals and if anyone expresses an interest in their sport, they are more than willing to help them get started; they will even lend their new friends equipment and spend hours teaching them. This may be how you got started, but if you want to make rapid progress and prevent instilling bad habits that will take a great deal of effort to correct, you are best off finding a good coach, from the beginning if possible.

What we are talking about now is finding a *personal* coach. The first coach you consult does not have to be an "elite coach" per se, but they do need to know something about training elite athletes. It would be nice to have a coach with more training (a USAA Level 3 or 4 coach or an NFAA Master Coach) but, at least at the beginning, that may not be necessary.

Your coach doesn't need to be a technical whiz or have experience coaching at the Olympic games. The key element in identifying your first coach is that person's ability to communicate with you and engage you in the kinds of things that are needed to be done for you to become a much better archer. As part of a rigorous study, very accomplished musicians were asked to rank their music teachers. They mostly ranked their first teachers as "average" (62%) or "better than average" (24%). The study concluded that these first teachers were selected from whomever was reasonably close and available (and affordable). So much for the idea that serious beginners need top notch coaching. These world-class musicians, though, characterized their first music teachers with words like "patient," "nice," and "she was really great with kids."

These first "coaches" were probably "average" in what the grownup music world looks at to rate teachers, but I think they were much better than that. They, like the New York cabbie who, when asked how to get to Carnegie Hall replied "Practice, Practice, Practice," were fully cognizant of the fact that a music teacher cannot be successful if she can't entice her students to practice. Many of these beginning piano teachers use charm and wiles to create a situation in which no student wanted to show up in her parlor not having practiced and incurring her disappointment. These beginning teachers were master, I don't want to say "motivators," maybe "encouragers" is a better word, but that is as close as I can get to what they were.

Finding a Good Coach

Unlike piano teachers, archery coaches don't take out ads in the yellow pages. Here are some steps you can try to locate a coach in your area.

1. If you have a local archery shop, ask them for a recommendation.
2. If you have an archery club in your area, ask them for a recommendation.
3. Try association websites. (USA Archery used to have a complete list of the coaches holding their advanced credentials, then it disappeared, but now I think it is back. Association contact info is provided in the Appendices.)
4. Attend a local archery competition and ask around.

This is a real problem that the archery community hasn't successfully addressed, yet. I would like to see a national registry of archery coaches that allows for archers and coaches to supply recommendations and evaluations (Angie's List for archers?).

When you ask for recommendations be sure to specify that you are not just looking for lessons for a beginning archer.

Lacking a good coach in your area, quite a few coaches are doing remote coaching now. Short video clips are taken of you shooting and are then emailed to the coach. The coach then replies with analysis and recommendations in follow-up phone (or Skype, etc.) sessions. This is not as good as live interaction between you and your coach, but it is better than nothing. If you find yourself in this situation, you can educate yourself so as to be able to better evaluate the information you are getting. In the Appendices, you will find some good books and videos that can help in this manner.

Do realize that coaches specialize. Some coaches are really good with compound bow archers buy don't have a clue about Olympic-style or Recurve Barebow archery, for example. It is really difficult to be good at coaching all styles. (I know, as I am trying to do just that and it is a daunting task; I am coming to the opinion there is too much to learn and experience to be really good at coaching all styles of archery. So, when I reach my limit, I look to pass on my students to a better coach, one who specializes in their style of archery.) So, ask your coach "What styles do you shoot/coach (or have you shot/coached)?" It is unlikely they will be very adept at any style they don't themselves practice (or have practiced). If what they shoot doesn't match your style of archery, ask them how many students they have had who shot your style. If they answer your question with "Oh, all styles." be very leery.

Ask About Your Coach's Training When you interview someone as to their availability to be your coach, do inquire into their training as a coach. My opinion is that you are better off with an instructor who has successfully completed a coach training course. Why? Well, coaching is really different from shooting. Shooting is all from a first person viewpoint and coaching is from a third person viewpoint. Archers are looking outward at their shot; coaches are looking inward. If your coach has taken a coach training course, at least they have made an effort toward becoming a better coach!

Does your coach having a current coaching certificate guarantee they are a good coach? No, but then neither does your lawyer having a law degree or doctor an M.D. degree guarantee you are working with a good lawyer or a good doctor. Having a valid, active coaching certificate means that your coach has received some training in how to teach and coach archery, which is a good thing.

Many archers equate being able to shoot arrows with the ability to teach others to shoot arrows, and they seek out the best archer they can find for "tips" or lessons. This is often the best of the available options, but it can be problematic. Imagine getting beginner golf lessons from a PGA Tour professional. They may not be able to connect their world to your world. They have vocabulary, awareness, and technique you may not be able to understand, let alone be able to emulate.

So, what kinds of coach trainings are there? Here's the problem. Most organizations either have no coach training programs or have a program different from the others. The good news is that the two most common certifications are now recognized by all of the major archery organizations. Here are descriptions of these trainings:

Basic Archery Instructor The Basic Archery Instructor training (also called a "Level 1" training) was designed to prepare nonarchers to assist in pre-existing archery programs. You do not need to know anything about archery to take this training, even though quite a few archers do. The reason most trainees aren't archers is that people who already are archers can skip to the next level of training (see immediately below) because much of this training is on how to shoot an arrow from a basic bow. The most common customer for such trainings are college students wanting jobs at summer camps and or as volunteer archery coaches at youth organization day camps. Most of these camp situations rotate their campers through a single archery session, so these instructors typically teach "Lesson 1" over and over again to kids who have never experienced archery.

The training lasts a single day and includes training on archery safety, archery terminology, and how to shoot an arrow as well as some rudimentary teaching techniques. There is a test that must be passed. I have participated in the training of scores of Level 1 archery instructors and I have never known anyone to not pass the test. You can take it that I am either a whiz of an archery instructor trainer or the test is relatively easy (or both).

Intermediate Archery Instructor The Intermediate Archery Instructor training (also called a "Level 2" training) is designed to prepare archers and holders of Basic Instructor/Level 1 certificates to run youth archery programs. You do need to know something about archery to take this training, because there is a pretest, testing the same knowledge as was taught in the Level 1 course. The most common customer for such trainings are archers wanting (or who got cajoled) to run an archery program at an archery range or shop. Here the instructor will be working with kids on an ongoing basis. (A typical format for these programs is 1-1.5 hour weekly or biweekly meetings and kids may start competing as part of a team representing that club.)

This training used to be 30 hours long, but is now two days, typically over a weekend. The topics include a safety review (always safety), more details on how to shoot arrows (shooting form and execution), more on teaching archery skills, and more on archery equipment (maintenance and adjustment). There is a test here, too. It is rare for anyone to fail it.

Okay, the bad news is that most Level 1 and Level 2 coaches will not be able to help you much, unless they are also very accomplished archers in your style of shooting.

More Advanced Trainings There are more advanced coach trainings, and they tend to be quite technical but the information and skills learned are more appropriate to your needs. Both my USA Archery Level 3 and Level 4 trainings were week-long sessions held at an Olympic training center. The trainers were very high level coaches and all of the bases got covered (nutrition, physical fitness, mental, technique, equipment, training, etc.). Each of these trainings required participants to pass an exit exam. In my Level 4 training (a combined Level 3/4 program), some candidates did not pass and were not given certificates.

The NFAA Master Coach program seems at present to be somewhat moribund, but in the past offered high level instruction.

Certificates Expire Most coach training certificates are for a period of time, for example three years or ten years. The point is made that if your instructing skills aren't exercised, they will diminish. Most of the organizations honoring these coaching certificates have a simple renewal policy that merely requires people to establish that they have been using their skills. Be aware, though, that there are a few who took a class 20 years ago and still claim to be a certified coach. Some archery knowledge evaporates quickly while other knowledge does not, so it is easy for us coaches to delude ourselves that we have "kept up" or that "nothing has really changed."

All certified instructors and coaches are given ID cards/certificates that are dated. It is not rude to ask to see it (or a facsimile).

What Does a Coach Cost?

I wish I could answer this question definitively. The best I can do is give you the same guidelines I recommend to coaches when the question: "What should I charge?" comes up.

Some Realities to Take Into Account Coaches fees need to conform to local standards. If a coach's cost of doing business are higher, they will need to have higher fees. But they are also constrained by how much people can and will pay for a service. Less affluent areas cannot afford the same fees as more affluent ones. You know this intuitively. You wouldn't go to the fanciest, most expensive golf course around if you were looking for cut-rate golf lessons, now would you? You also can't ask people from other states what they get charged for their lessons and get numbers that can be assumed to be good for your locale. I'm not saying you shouldn't collect such data, just that you need to keep the above in mind to evaluate it.

And what you are charged is more than a just fee; it says something about the value or quality of what is being charged for. Let me tell you a story I heard in my USA Archery Level 3 Coach training class. A JOAD (Junior Olympic Archery Development) coach participating noticed one of his archers had stopped coming to lessons. When he encountered that student's mother in the community, he expressed disappointment that the student was no longer in archery. The mom, on the other hand, told him that they had simply changed over and attending another JOAD program. When the coach inquired as to why, the mom indicated that, well, he only charged $1 per lesson, while the other program charged $6. The coach and his program advisors thought that they were lowering barriers to participation by only charging a nominal $1 per lesson to cover the costs of target faces, etc. What they ran up against was a clash of perceived values. In our culture, we associate price with quality. If something is very inexpensive, it is not expected to be also of high quality. Conversely, if it is of high quality, it is not expected to be inexpensive. A $6 per lesson class has to be better than a $1 per lesson class, no?

So, some of the things that must be taken into account are:

1. local standards
2. perceived values

and . . . well, there are more but these are enough for now.

Fees for Individual Coaching Sessions There are a number of ways fees might be set for individual coaching sessions, so we are going to look at several of them instead of just one. For "one offs" or one-time-only coaching sessions, you may have to pay more or less. Expect to negotiate the fee.

Fees Based on a Training Standard In this case fees are based on the training the coach brings to the table. As an example, here is one based on USA Archery's older coach training scheme:

Level 2 Coach	$25/hour
Level 3 Coach	$35/hour
Level 4 Coach	$45/hour
Elite Coach	$55/hour and up (to be negotiated)

Elite coaches not uncommonly charge $100-$125 per hour. These values are based on informal surveys taken in 2008 and might then have been adjusted for inflation or deflation (and, of course, local standards).

You will find these values significantly less than average fees for golf, tennis, or even swimming coaches. I know that elite baseball hitting instructors can charge $125 for a half-hour lesson without batting an eye (a little baseball humor there).

The weakness of this system is, of course, how do you equate one organization's training to another's. And, your coach may have gotten a Level 3 certificate from USA Archery as a recurve bow specialist, but that doesn't mean he or she knows much at all about compound bows.

Fees Based on Accomplishments—These could be archery accomplishments (Former world champion!) or coaching accomplishments (Over the past ten years, I have coached 112 archery champions!). I do not have enough experience with fees set this way to come up with an approximate fee structure based on such criteria, but since so many coaches brag about such things, they might be a criterion.

Fees Based on Archer Level—In this scheme, the fees involved are based on the level the archer is at. Here is an example:

Beginning Archer	$25/hour
Intermediate Archer	$35/hour
Advanced Archer	$45/hour
Elite Archer	$55/hour and up (to be negotiated)

I am afraid I just made up these figures as I have no surveys or other data upon which to base estimates.

The idea here is to match the fee to the knowledge and expertise a coach needs to work with an archer of a particular level. For example, bow-arrow system tuning does not come up in lessons of beginning archers. Maybe bare shaft tune checking comes up for intermediate archers. But, for elite archers, coaches had better be more than a little knowledgeable about a wide array of tuning methods if they want to work with folk like you. And since you aspire to be an elite archer, these are the coaches you need to zoom in on.

The odds are probably better than even that your coach has no better idea what to charge you than you do, so don't be afraid to discuss your coach's fee with him/her. There are no national or other standards, so that means any fee is subject to negotiation. (Which also means that I am free to charge clients who are rude or abrasive a higher fee!)

On behalf of all archery coaches, though, please realize that the odds are very good that archery coaches fees are less than are the coaching fees for most other sports. There is also a long standing attitude that we shouldn't charge kids at all for lessons in the sport. I won't argue that notion here, but do realize that it puts downward pressure on the fees coaches tend to charge. So, if the fee sounds reasonable to you, it probably is, and more so.

Managing Your Life

If you do everything you can to become a winning archer and lose your family or your spouse or your job or a college degree, through selfless dedication to winning, I must question whether you have won anything at all. I define success only in the context of a life well-lived. Sacrifices are needed to achieve excellence in anything but I strongly urge you to consider the costs when making important decisions.

I knew a spectacular young man who rose to the rank of being the #2 rated Olympic-style archer in the U.S. He shot all through school including college. He took many months out of his life to train full-time at the Olympic Training Center. At the Olympic Trials he was set on winning or placing to become an Olympian, he had an inexplicable "bad day." One bad day and he missed making the team. Shortly thereafter he went to graduate school. I haven't seen his name on a competitive roster since. Was it worth it to him? I haven't had the heart to ask him.

Rick McKinney, three-time World Champion and two-time Olympic Silver Medalist, has frankly shared his story of suffering a severe depression after winning his first world championship. What does one do when one works obsessively to achieve and then meets one's life goal . . . at the age of 23? Are you prepared for this? Is anyone prepared for this? I will share what Rick learned below.

If you take care of all of the technical and mental and other skills needed to be proficient enough to win and win big, you still won't win unless you have mastered the other aspects of your life as well. Athletes in personal turmoil rarely perform well. Athletes inspired by personal challenges often achieve greatness.

Sacrifices Athletes have to sacrifice a great deal to achieve the status of being a consistent winner. Often, you have little time for much of anything outside the home but work or school and practice or competition. If you are very young, it is a bad idea to specialize in a sport to the exclusion of all other activities. It is bad for you in many ways, including bad for your archery. Who we are as an archer is informed by who we are as a person, and specializing on just one sport and mildly obsessing on it cuts you off from a great many other influences that could shape your life.

If you are not young, and you are balancing the demands of having to earn a living and the demands of family, try to be as organized as you can be. Include family time in your plans. Don't make your sacrifice their sacrifice, too.

Having said all of the above, family and friends will have to sacrifice some things if you seriously pursue the goal of becoming a winning archer. You won't be at a nephew's birthday party, because you have to practice. You might miss a child's soccer game because you are at a tournament. Be aware of what they are sacrificing, because as Lanny Bassham says, there must be payback. It may not happen until you retire or take a year off from serious competition, but your friends and family have been doing without you because of your endeavor, you owe them more of you (than you are inclined to give, in all probability) afterward or during the "off season" to compensate for this. Too many people find the cost of pursuing competitive excellence is lost friends, broken promises, and divorce. Don't make this mistake.

McKinney's Lesson I mentioned Rick McKinney's story above, namely that of achieving his life's goal at a very early age. The "is that all there is" feeling can be very profound, especially because, in archery, there isn't financial wealth at the end of the trail. Athletes in football and basketball and baseball can "win" professional careers including immense salaries, which means they can do pretty much what they want for the rest of their lives. Archers aren't competing for anywhere near that much money. Rick's lesson, discovered through no little personal pain, was to never have just an ultimate goal, you have to think beyond all of your goals. So, what if you become World Champion, then what? What if you win the Vegas Shoot and the biggest monetary reward available to archers? What then?

And I think you need to take his lesson farther. What about after archery? After competition? What is meaningful to you? Do you want to become a coach? Do you want to transform archery equipment? What else do you want to do in your life?

Having a balanced life should be the outcome of any particular life pursuit. There will be forces urging you to spend more time on your sport, and forces urging you to do the opposite. Your task is to balance these demands and find the energy to meet your goals . . . all of them.

Good luck and enjoy!

Key Points
Chapter 9 Developing Your Support Team

You might just make it doing everything yourself, but why do it the hard way?

- In general, behind every successful archer there is a support team.
- The members of your support team, if they are family, sacrifice a great deal of their time with you for you to pursue winning archery. You need to include some payback time doing things with them that they want to do. And you need to appreciate what they do for you and communicate that appreciation to them.
- Finding a good personal coach will probably not be easy.
- Coaches specialize. Be sure the one you are looking at has experience with the style you shoot.
- Training to be a coach is quite different from training to be an archer.
- Many, if not most, coaches got their training as "on the job training," you are probably best off if you are not one of the students providing your coach OJT.
- It is reasonable to ask a coach about his/her training and to see their certificates. (They are dated.)
- Expect to pay your coach. A free coach may or may not be helpful but it is really hard for an archer to put demands on a coach who is working for free.
- Being a winning archer is only part of your life. If you neglect the rest and focus only on archery, much sadness is in your future.

10

Competing to Win

So, you are prepared to win. Your practice scores are right where they need to be. Your mental program is strong and practiced until it is fairly automatic. You have made your travel and lodging arrangements. The competition is three days away, now what?

Actually, what winners do is rather straightforward and simple. But, let's start with what you do *not* want to do. Certainly it would be foolish to tinker with your equipment, form, or execution at this point as there is not enough time to make any such changes into anything but problems. As just one example, I decided to tie a bottom nocking point onto my bowstring right before the NFAA Outdoor Nationals one year. On the 15 yard Field target one day I managed a 15(3X) score. You guessed it, my fourth arrow was off of the target because, in a moment of distraction, I nocked that arrow below the bottom nocking point instead of below the top one. I had not gotten used to the existence of that bottom nocking point yet.

You also don't want arduous shooting marathons at this point as you want to be physically and mentally fresh at the competition. And you do not want to shoot practice scoring rounds this close to actual competition. If you shoot a good score, what does it tell you? Nothing you did not already know. But a poor score shot on an "off day" can be a major source of doubt, leading to a lack of confidence, which is not at all helpful.

What you do want to do is twofold: you want to rehearse mentally and you want to stay sharp but be relaxed. The key part of this is that *winners always have a routine they follow*. This routine is whatever works for you, but the "sameness" of it is something that is comforting. All competitors who are successful have some sort of pre-game routine. Baseball players and golfers are notorious for carrying such things to extremes. Basketball players do the same. Archers are no different. Let's look at this in more detail.

The Mental Part of Pre-Competition Prep

The mental part of pre-competition preparation involves imagery: basically you want to imagine yourself in the venue competing and, of course, competing well in the days leading up to the competition. For this imagery to be effective, you want to include the sights, the sounds (crowd noise, the distinctive noise of arrows hitting targets indoors, the twangs of bowstrings), the smells (freshly mown grass, mountain air, the smell of rain, the flinty scent of desert sand, the smoke from a barbeque pit) in as much detail as you can muster. On the first day of competition, you want it to feel like day three.

The reason for this is simple. In my first NFAA nationals (five days, 4 arrows per target, 28 targets per day) I shot a poor score on Day 1. On Day 2, I shot better. Also better on Days 3, 4, and 5. Day 5 (the Animal Round) was highlighted by a personal best score. This is not atypical of one's first tournament at a new venue. (I had never even been to the State of Washington before.) All of the sights, the sounds, the weather, the climate (and the bugs) were new. One of the big advantages of experience is having been to a venue beforehand and knowing what to expect (wind, weather, sights, sounds, temperature, bugs, mud, food).

If you have never been to a venue before, ask your friends if they have pictures from a previous shoot. Check the Internet for pictures of the venue. The web sites of a number of field clubs now display photos of all of their targets from the vantage of the farthest shooting stake and include descriptions of whether the target is shot uphill, downhill, or sidehill. Once you have some images, become a movie director: add sound, people, special effects in your imagination. If the venue is not that far away, consider going there and shooting a practice round some time before the event (as close in time as you can arrange it but allowing for practice time to work on issues that might arise). Your mind can do wonders with just scraps of information, but the wealth of information you get from having competed on a field before is invaluable. For example, one year prior to any Olympic Games, they have what is called a "test event." It is an actual competition on the field that will be used for the Games. This gives the organizers a chance to test their systems and the competitors a chance to experience what it is like competing on that field. Of course, poor countries often can't afford to send a team, putting them at somewhat of a disadvantage. If you can't afford to go ahead of time to practice at a venue, you too are at somewhat of a disadvantage.

Consequently, winning a competition the first time you actually compete in it is rather rare (except in the kid's brackets as there is a great deal of turnover and last year's winners may not come this year or may have moved up in age class, virtually guaranteeing someone else will win). The lesson for you is that the first time you go to compete in an event or in an event that has a new venue, you are probably better off setting modest goals, focusing on execution, etc. and if you happen to win, it is even more wonderful for being unexpected. In any case, take notes! Some people do this mentally, but I suggest you keep a competition log. At the end of every day, make note of the conditions (weather, good or poor lighting (especially indoors), quality of the organization, everything) and make notes of things you did well and things you would like to have done differently. Generally I ask my students to make the latter two lists ("Things I Did Well" and "Things I Will Do Differently Next Time") with at least three items on each list for each and every competition they attend. The list of things that you would like to do differently provides direction for subsequent practices, and your comments on the venue will help if you attend the next time. These notes will help your memory create your preparatory visualizations. It doesn't hurt to take some photos, even videos, of the venue. It is better if you can get your coach, spouse, or other member of your support team to do this for you as pictures and/or videos of you competing are helpful and passing this task off allows you to concentrate just on your shooting.

The Physical Part of Pre-Competition Prep

Physically, there can be a lot of planning involved. If you are traveling to a foreign country, I recommend you inquire as to the food available. If the cuisine of that country is not agreeable (e.g. it is famous for its seafood and you don't eat seafood), you are going to want to research where you can eat agreeable food. You may have to go to grocery stores and buy ingredients to cook yourself.

If there is jet lag involved, you do not want to be flying in the morning of a competition. Also, just sitting for hours in an airplane can be debilitating for an athletic performance.

If at all possible, I arrive at least a day early to get some practice in on site. Many competitions do not allow you to practice on the competitive field prior to the event but almost always provide a practice range for you to use. I go through my full warm-up routine (see below) and then check my sight marks. When I am shooting compound, I am somewhat loathe to make any adjustments during this practice, because all of my marks were perfect when I left home. But there are conditions under which your sight marks might have changed a little: if you left a very hot weather place and went to a cold weather place; if you left a very dry place and went to a damp place (or vice-versa), if you left a low elevation place and went to a high elevation place (or vice-versa), for example. But any such changes should be small. You can read about people who had to make dramatic adjustments between venues, but with modern bows, there is much less in the way of natural products incorporated in bow limbs and such and there is less temperature and humidity response accordingly. There is more of an effect with recurve bows than compound bows and, again, the effects were greater with older bows. When I compete with a longbow, because I favor a non-laminated bow, the weather/temperature effects are greater and I adjust accordingly and without hesitation.

This pre-competition practice is not a long session, but I want to take full note of the footing (slopes, mud, solid ground/grass), lighting (sun or artificial), and the wind (direction, strength, consistent or swirling). Conditions may be different the next day (and often are) but there is no sense in ignoring information that may be helpful.

Just Before the Competition Begins For the first day at a new venue, you are going to want to arrive a half hour to an hour earlier than you would to an ordinary competition. While you may have learned the route to the event on a practice day (I love MapQuest), the traffic may be entirely different on the competition day. All kinds of things may take time you didn't expect (equipment inspections, finding the portapotties, connecting with long lost friends you didn't expect to see, there may be lines at the practice targets, etc.).

Before I start shooting I want to do some light aerobic warm-up (a brisk walk, for example) and a short warm-up routine. When I begin shooting, I like to do so on a blank bale. If one isn't available, I will often shoot off target initially. I always start shooting with two let downs—I fully execute my shot sequence and then let down. I am covering two things by doing this: I am waking up my "shooting self" and I am reinforcing the fact that a let down is always an option. I will let down a couple of more times during warm-up shooting and then again during official practice (if any) for the second reason. I want to avoid shooting at a target initially because if I miss my first shot, I immediately get into error correction mode (What did I do wrong? Did I mis-set my sight? etc.). Before I shoot at a target, I want to be sure all of the correct muscle groups are activated and functioning and my mental program is up and running. This only takes a half dozen shots or so. Then I will shoot at a target. If I am warming up for a field shoot, I will shoot some arrows at relatively short distance, and some at a longer distance (though not usually the longest distance) as I am warming up and just checking to see if I am functioning well. I checked all of my marks the day before so I am not testing them.

A Few Precautions There is a potential downside to having a pre-competition routine. I am sure you realize that things do not always go as planned. If you let disruptions to your warm-up routine throw you off of your game, you are undermining your own chances of winning. Disruptions of routine are normal, approach them that way. Do not get upset over them, just deal with the disruption and get back into your routine. If you do show a proclivity to let little things upset you, do not be surprised that there are some competitors who will arrange to make sure that those little things are often thrown your way. While the vast majority of competitors are worthy of respect, there is a small number who feel that playing "mind games" is a fair way to get a competitive advantage. If you have a hissy fit over something small, the odds are good the story will get around and then the odds are also good that folks who feel it is "fair game" to disrupt your routine will find a way to do it regularly.

Your routine, whatever it turns out to be, is a support, not a crutch. Whenever something is not handled by your routine, have a quiet thought of appreciation for the things that it does do, and move on. A story is told of Tiger Woods, who was not happy with his warm-up session which had begun about ten minutes earlier. He returned all of his clubs to his bag and started over, from the beginning. There was certainly no advantage in getting upset and starting over might have gotten him into his pre-competition routine more successfully. Of course, there has to be the time available to do this.

Let the Competition Begin

The "habits" of winning archers tend to be very detailed. Consider arrows as an example. The penalty for not shooting all of the arrows in an end is very severe. You lose the points you could have scored with those arrows. The penalty for shooting extra arrows can also be severe. The rules vary but typically you lose at least the score of the highest scoring arrow in the target. So, you will find that top archers have a *quiver routine*. Mine involves the fact I use a four tube quiver. If the shoot has three arrow ends, I put two arrows in the top tube and one arrow in the second tube, the third tube is empty and the fourth has defective arrows (usually upside down in the tube) and spare arrows. By loading the quiver this way, all I need do is look at my quiver and I can tell exactly how many arrows I have shot: if I see two arrows in the top tube I have shot none; if I see one arrow in the top tube I have shot one; if I have one arrow in the second tube, I have shot two; if no arrows in the top three tubes, I am done. And I don't really have to count, a glance will tell, just like you know which side of a dice cube is up by glancing and not counting the pips.

Similarly, in a five arrow shoot, I put three arrows in the top tube and two in the second. For six arrow shoots I generally put two arrows in each of the top three tubes. I always shoot from the "top" of the stack down. I never shoot arrows from the fourth tube. If I am replacing a damaged arrow, I take a spare and place it in its proper tube to be taken out in its normal sequence. When my hand drops to my quiver, I am always selecting arrows in the right order, that is from the top down.

Additionally, each of my arrows is numbered in such a way that the numbers aren't visible when the arrows are nocked on my bowstring. The arrows are numbered because if I have an arrow that doesn't seem to be grouping well, I can keep track of it by its number. The arrow numbers are hard to see because I don't want any doubt to creep into any of my shots. (Oh, darn, here's that arrow that isn't grouping well!) Some archers do the opposite; they mark arrows for good shots so when they nock that arrow, all of the "good shot marks" lend a sense of confidence to the shot.

Arrows have to be inspected each time they are shot. Elsewhere in this book I told a story of what happened to me in a shoot in which I shot an arrow with no point in it (it didn't score). This would have been noticed during even a casual inspection, had I done one. If you shoot all-carbon arrows, most manufacturers suggest you check them for cracks after each shot. Loose vanes can cost you a point. Cracked nocks can cost you points and even the arrow and sometimes a bow. (An arrow with a cracked nock can result in a dry fire which breaks the bow.)

All of these checks can be done while walking back to the shooting line or on to the next target, but they need to be done. The only way you can avoid failing to remember to do these checks is to make a habit of them. You have to do them religiously until you don't have to think about doing them. It also pays to deliberately focus on these checks during your warm ups so the habit will be triggered before you start scoring.

When shooting field courses, I have a habit I created because of points I lost from mis-setting my sight. When I walk to a new shooting stake, I set my sight to the new distance. When it is my turn to shoot, when I step to the shooting line, I check the distance and my sight setting. I do not mis-set my sight anymore because of this "double check" habit.

The routines you come up with will be, to some extent, by trial and error as we don't all make the same kinds of mistakes. But, when you do encounter a mental mistake (one that can be cured by some thought), you need to take some time and think about how to avoid that problem again. It may require you to create a new habit to keep it in check.

Dealing With Rule Violations There will be occasions when someone in your competitive group violates one of the rules of competition. I have always found that it is best to address these lapses when they come up, instead of waiting until a round is over and filing a complaint. The best way to do this, in my opinion, is to merely ask a question: "Doesn't the rule say. . . ?" or "Isn't it the case that. . . ?" This sounds less accusatory and will be less embarrassing to you if you mistake the application of the rule.

In the vast majority of such cases, following a bit of discussion, compliance with the rules of competition is arranged. At USA Archery events, there are judges on the field who can be approached for clarifications and some of the field events have range officials able to give clarifications in real time.

I remember spotting arrows in a field competition, mostly for my own amusement. Everyone knows (and now you do, too) that if someone spots arrows for you, they are under no obligation to say anything and if you ask them the position of the arrow just shot, they are not responsible for any mistakes they might make. You are responsible for spotting your own arrows, period. But in major NFAA competitions, the smaller targets are put up in sets of four, the number of archers in a group, and if you shoot from the left side of the stake, you shoot a left-hand target, if you shoot first line, you shoot the bottom row (to prevent shadows of arrows shot on top interfering with aiming at lower targets). And, most importantly, if you shoot the wrong target, the arrow doesn't score. There was an occasion where a shooting partner shot the wrong target. I have heard stories of archers just watching as their competitor proceeded to shoot the next three into the wrong target also. But, the rules are one thing and courtesy is another. After seeing the wrong target being shot, I suggested that the archer in question check to see if he were shooting the correct target. He was very grateful for the correction, shooting his next three arrows for score.

Courtesy toward other competitors is something I expect from my students and I recommend to you. I have been graced many, many times by fellow competitors who straightened me out on rules and etiquette during shoots (possibly made easier because I was clearly no threat at the time, but still . . .).

Dealing with Rule Violators (Cheaters) When someone refuses compliance or who is clearly violating the rules to their betterment, you may not be dealing with ignorance, but with cheating. This is exceedingly rare but it does happen. And this can be very difficult to deal with because confrontations with cheaters can be very upsetting. In general, you need to deal with this in your group or call in an official.

If the group can deal with it, fine; if not, do not hesitate to call in officials. That is what they are there for (in part, of course).

What you cannot let happen is having the problem upset you and prevent you from shooting your game.

Dealing with Equipment Disasters I remember competing in the Pacific Coast Championships one year and on my next to last shot in one end, the rope on my release broke. (This was before D-loops.) I checked my quiver only to find that I hadn't stuck my backup release in my pouch (oops). So, I walked back to my chair, found my equipment bag, dug out my backup release, walked back to the line and shot my last arrow.

A really cool customer, no? Actually, no. I am a rather nervous person. But I hate shooting makeup arrows because they are out of context, so I wanted to avoid having to do that. What gave me license to do what I did was I keep a countdown timer on my spotting scope tripod while I am shooting. I had over a minute and a half left (of a four minute end), so I knew I had the time to get back to the line with plenty of time to take the shot. This allowed me to relax and get the job done.

Obviously if this had been a field tournament and my backup release aid (or a replacement rope) hadn't been in my quiver, I would have been in much deeper doo doo. The rules do allow for equipment repairs, but they are severely time limited and it is usually a very long walk back to the starting point where the rest of your stuff can be found.

It is important that you know the rules regarding equipment failures. If you stand at a shooting stake holding your bow overhead at an NFAA field tournament, your fellow competitors will think you are nuts. That is a signal one would use at a USA Archery sponsored tournament. It signals a judge to come over, verify your equipment failure, and arrange for your makeup arrows (time and place) to be shot. Every organization has different rules. You need to know these.

Backup Equipment I had been in archery quite a while before I had the luxury of having a backup bow. I tend to start my young recurve students trying out competition with the idea of acquiring a backup tab. Tabs are small and easy to lose. My partner Claudia is famous in California for losing her tab in a portapotty (yes, in the worst place) in the midst of a major competition. She also had no backup tab! The story has a happy ending because her competitors cobbled together a makeshift tab for her (which wasn't easy as she is left-handed) and she went on to win (although blowing almost all of a 30+ point lead). Another fine example of archery courtesy.

After acquiring a backup tab (or release aid), the next thing needed is a backup bowstring. This, like all backup equipment, must be "shot in" and ready to swap in for what you need it to replace. For recurve archers, backup limbs can be used, but the Roll Royce (Cadillac, Lexus, whatever) of backup equipment is a backup bow. While you can strip your old bow of its stabilizers, sights, and whatnot, having a complete backup setup (bow, sight, stabilizers, etc., even arrows) is superior because there are no two bows that are exactly identical. You can order two brand new bows from the same manufacturer, having the same specs, and demanding that the parts be made on the same days . . . and those two bows will be slightly different, to the point that they will feel slightly different and have slightly different sight marks. If you take two identically set up bows and blindfold a top archer, he or she can tell the difference between the two from shooting them, sight unseen. Take away one bow and give them the other one, they will tell you that you have given them a different bow. Take away one bow and give it right back to them and they will be able to tell that you gave them the same bow back.

So, having a complete backup bow with sight, stabilizers, etc. gives you a setup that can be shot in, sighted in, and you can be comfortable with it. More importantly, you can trust it to be what it is. Consequently if a cable on your #1 bow starts to go, or the riser cracks, etc. you can just swap it out for your backup setup and you are good to go. The only thing you have to deal with is the fact that you think of your backup bow as your No. 2 Bow. (If you thought it was better than the other one, it would have been your No. 1 Bow.) Shooting your backup bow, that you set up, that you shot in and tuned, that you sighted in is therefore no big deal. But, when you get an opportunity to shoot it in competition, think positively about how you are going to learn how Bow #2 does under those circumstances. And, a number of people have discovered that what they thought was their No. 2 Bow turned out to be really their No. 1 Bow. Don't cheat it out of its debut!

Also, if there is a required equipment inspection, you do know to get your back-up bow/arrows inspected, don't you?

Competition Day Management

If you are participating in The Vegas Shoot, your "day" is thirty arrows shot in under a couple of hours. You do not need to plan on managing your meals, hydration, weather gear, etc. You do, though, need to show up on time. Every archer I know has several stories of archers who slept through their start times. In today's paper there was a story of a PGA golfer who overslept his start time for the pro-am event preceding the Tour event he was entered in. Even though this was not a competitive event, the penalty was disqualification from the weekend tournament, which just happened to be the first leg of the FedEx Cup playoffs!

In archery, the odds that there will be someone you entrust with your wakeup time are poor. I do not even trust a hotel "wake-up call." I carry a travel alarm and set both the room's alarm clock (or wake-up call) and my own alarm. I like it best that I am awake and moving around when the front desk calls (or the hotel clock alarm buzzer sounds). And you need to double and triple check your shoot time.

You absolutely need to have a good breakfast on competition day. The ideas of what constitutes a "good breakfast" are all over the map but I tend to agree with Barry Groves ("Eat Fat, Get Thin," 2000) who happens also to be an archer, that you are better off with a breakfast higher in fat and protein (bacon and eggs, etc.) than one loaded with carbohydrates (pancakes, waffles, syrup, etc.). If you are one of those people who are too nervous to eat or don't like to eat before an early stating time, you will have a adapt accordingly. What you don't want to do is start your competitive day on an empty fuel tank (or for that matter, an over full one).

There is tremendous amounts of misinformation about being "hydrated" at a sporting event. Some of this is utter nonsense ("you need to drink eight 8-oz glasses of water a day") while other is good advice for another competitor on another field. If I were doing a decathlon on a stadium floor covered with synthetic turf with a predicted high temperature of 108°F in the shade of which there is none, I would recommend large quantities of fluids being taken quite often. Archers shooting indoors for 1-2 hours are really unlikely to become dehydrated. I have a bottle of one of the sports drinks, diluted 50:50 with water handy in case I want to drink something. The diluted sports drink is what I drink for those Sacramento, CA outdoor shoots in 100+°F weather. It just speaks "competition" to me, so I drink it indoors, too. (There is some scientific evidence that a diluted sports drink is taken up faster than the full strength stuff.)

You'll have to make up your own mind on caffeine. Some avoid it like the plague, others say they need it to be able to compete. The science is somewhat divided.

Archery is a low impact, low arousal, endurance event. Shooting a full FITA Round or a 28-target field competition can take anywhere from 4-8 hours. One year at the NFAA Marked 3-D Tournament in Redding, California, Claudia and I got to our first shooting stake at 7:30 a.m. We got back to our vehicle at 7:00 p.m. This was only a two-arrow shoot of 40 targets, but each target had 20-30 people in line ahead of us so we had to wait, and wait, and wait at each target and it was very hot. We ran though all of the hydration fluids we had with us and bought a great deal more throughout the day. The same was true for the food we took along.

You must plan out your snacks, meals, and beverages ahead of time if you don't want to be caught off guard. In California, our field events were often accompanied by the availability of great food being prepared by the host. But, if you depend on it entirely (and many folks do) and they run out or they run out of food you would eat and are only left with food you find undesirable, you are in trouble. If you like to just show up with "lunch money" in your pocket, make sure you note whether your performance suffers after eating or whether, later in the day, you "ran out of gas." If this strategy doesn't work for you, don't use it!

On the target field, you have the luxury of having a cooler or "ice chest" available. In these circumstances, I tend to have bottles of diluted sports beverages (50:50 with water) on hand (The straight stuff has too much sugar and doesn't get absorbed as quickly.) and which I sip regularly. There is no sense in getting even close to being dehydrated while competing. I tend to have baggies of cut up cheeses, vegetables, and deli meats. All are "finger food" so they are easy to eat and are high in protein, with little carbohydrate. This keeps me on an even keel all day long.

During field events, it is different. You have to carry everything with you. Consequently I forego all of the perishable foods and take "nutrition bars" with me.

They are lightweight and filling and are the best I can do under the circumstances. I also carry a refillable water bottle, as "water stations" at field events are not always reliable, but when they are, I want to be able to refill my empties. If I am expecting high temperatures and exposure to the sun, I will carry two water bottles. I also carry a collapsible lightweight stool, as many of these events have little to no seating available at targets and it is desirable to rest from time to time (more so now that I am in my 60's than it was 30 years ago).

If the sun is bright, will you be wearing sunglasses? Did you bring them? Have you practiced shooting in them? If you wear prescription glasses, did you bring spares? (I broke my glasses at one event.) If you wear contacts, did you bring replacements and some solution with you? If this is a target event, then generally you are close to your vehicle to get things you have forgotten. But at a field event, you may be a mile and half from the clubhouse/parking lot when you lose a contact lens, and you are not going to win that competition without a replacement.

Tournament Nerves

I am somewhat a nervous person, so I have accumulated a number of things to deal with nervousness associated with competition. If you are "Cool Hand Luke" with ice water in your veins and never suffer from nervousness, skip to the next section.

Nerves associated with performing are natural but can be upsetting. The good news is there are ways to deal with them. The biggest cure for nerves is experience. Having shot the same tournament ten times will provide you with a far different set of feelings than those from your first time. (For one, all of the ways you could imagine you could embarrass yourself would have either proved unfounded or you would have them done and out of the way.)

If you don't have experience, there are a number of ways to fake it. For one, during warm up or practice ends just prior to the start of the tournament, you can imagine the competition already started. By the time the first scoring end comes around, you are already on End 3. If your powers of imagining are good, you can imagine you are shooting at home or your club's range instead of where you are. The experience you have at that venue will translate (some).

If you are in a shoot off and you find yourself really quite nervous, try "The Fake Yawn." I learned this from the Basshams and it really works. Just up and yawn, really wide. We usually yawn when we are tired or bored, both of which are not very excited states. The yawning, even though it is faked, creates some of that calmness for you.

The hardcore realists love the feeling of tournament nerves, because it means they are close, close to that winner's circle. You don't get that feeling from finishing in 35th place. They think of being nervous as a reward for shooting well.

I have to tell you a story. The very first time I was in a shoot off, it was for my field archery club's championship. (The only reason I was even tied for first is the contest was handicapped.) Our shoot off was, by rule, a three target contest. My handicap gave me an extra 1.25 points per 20 point target. Unfortunately my two opponents were several (many, actually) time state, national, and even world champions. The first target was the 80-70-60-50 yard walkup (one arrow at each distance scored 5-4-3). I had been told that in a shoot off it was to your advantage to shoot first, so I confidently (as confidently as I could) stepped up to the shooting stake with the other two with the intent of getting off the first arrow. I was shaking so much I could barely see the target through my scope and I wasn't sure my release would go off. The scorer (with binoculars) calls my arrow "It's a three." A three? I was upset. I was more than upset, I actually got somewhat mad. I finished that target 5-5-5 for an 18 and shot the next two targets as well or better and won the contest without even needing my handicap.

What I learned was that when I am very nervous, it doesn't hurt me to build up a bit of a head of steam. The other guys were as calm as cucumbers—they had experience, lots of it. Even with experience I don't become that calm, so being a little shaky is "normal" for me and doesn't affect my ability to score. (I shook like a leaf for every one of the 12 shots I took in that shoot off.)

I also learned that all pressure is self-imposed. We put it on ourselves. Nobody does it to us. The situation doesn't do it to us. We do it to ourselves. So, if you are struggling with shooting nerves, ask yourself "What's the best thing that could happen? What's the worse thing that could happen? What could happen if I just relaxed and shot as if I didn't care too much about the outcome?" These questions bring out the reality of the situation. You are not shooting for your life or your mother's life or something really important. It is an archery contest, after all. Often unnamed fears and anticipations are the source of such nerves. Mentally imagine yourself waving to the crowd when introduced, shaking hands with the other competitors, then shooting perfect shots. And, what the heck, imagine yourself getting that first place medal (and a check if there is one). It will be as if you had done it all before and we all know what experience does for one's nerves.

Disaster Management

In 2006 Dave Cousins showed up in Göteborg, Sweden for the FITA World Field Championships. Unfortunately, his bow, arrows, release aids, and optics failed to make it with him. Guess who was in first place after Day 1 of the competition? Yep, Mr. Cousins. He borrowed a teammate's backup bow, some arrows, and a release aid from others and sighted in. It would be a greater story if he had won the whole thing, but he didn't, he "only" came in second! What he did accomplish, though, seems like a miracle. It's not. You can come close to this kind of performance.

The topic here is what are you going to do when things go awry? Do you have a plan? Do you know what to do?

The Smallest Thing Let's start with the smallest disaster. A little disaster. Let's say you are right there, with a little luck or a slip by your opponent and you're going to win this tournament. Then the unthinkable happens: you are the one who makes a mistake. You are distracted, worse, you started thinking about winning and you make a bad shot. You've have probably just shot yourself out of a win. What do you do?

The most important thing to realize is that you can't do a thing about the arrow you just shot. You can't do a thing by analyzing what you did wrong (at least not right then). You can, though, regain your poise, find your shot, and make the next shot a really good shot and finish the tournament with no more mistakes. The techniques to do this are already known to you: you must let go of the last shot, you must relax (deep breaths help), and you must get right back into your shot sequence, both physically and mentally.

"What's the point? I just blew a win," you ask?

The point is, you don't know that your opponent won't make an even more damaging mistake. He might have noticed your poor shot, relaxed mentally and lost focus, and is about to put you right back into the fight for first. Even if he makes no mistake, it is imperative you practice recovering from mistakes. If you blow up and make several mistakes in a row because you are mad at yourself, you are practicing doing just that the next time this happens. And, mistakes are often made early in a competition when you have time to catch up from what you have just given away. You need to be able to get back into your sequence and rhythm as a matter of course. You need to think about "the next time."

Later, you need to analyze what happened to cause that mistake, so you understand what happened and can recognize when it might happen again, because you may be able to prevent that mistake in the future. But that is for when the tournament is over. (Don't wait more than 24 hours to think about it analytically, as you will lose all connection to what really happened.)

Having a "recovery routine" is a good strategy. First, you must stop thinking about the mistake. You must think about something else: a yappy little dog, a favorite movie, anything as long as it is different from the poor shot you just made. Next, you must do something physical, like jostling the arrows in your quiver or tapping your bow or resettling your binoculars, something physical that gets you out of the realm of the entirely mental, then you need to begin the process of engaging the next shot. If you use "cue words" like: "follow through" or "let it (your aperture) float" such cues can get you mentally into the next shot. According to Troy Bassham of Mental Management Systems, this process needs to take at least seven seconds, so don't just rush into your next shot thinking to wipe away the memory of the bad shot with the image of a good one. Resetting mentally takes a bit of time. Spend a little time in practice on your recovery routine and the next time you make a mistake, execute your strategy and get back on track. (I know I have said this before but as I told you, I don't count on you having read that bit before!)

Dealing with a Bigger Problem I remember sitting in a booth at a USA Archery Outdoor Nationals and a young man who I coached a bit from time to time dropped into a chair right next to me and said: "I suck!" He hadn't shot at all well on the first two days of the competition. My response was "Good!" He looked at me as if I were crazy. I explained that he now had an opportunity to learn how to "grind." Grinding is what golfers do when they don't have their best day on the course. The idea is to not give away any more shots than is absolutely necessary so that if their game comes back to them, they will still be high enough on the leader board to make the cut, get a paycheck, finish in the top twenty, whatever. One tournament does not make a season or a career. Archers need to learn to grind, also. Some tournaments last several days and mistakes can be overcome.

If something has gone really wrong, you have the opportunity to practice your troubleshooting, exercise all of your mental skills, try out your backup bow in competition . . . the list is endless. There is a great deal to learn in these situations. Or, you could just mope and gripe and miss out entirely. A number of professional archers I have known were notorious for stomping off when they dropped out of contention, going home early, usually in a huff. Some quite famous archers are also famous for temper tantrums involving bows wrapped around trees, etc.

It is your choice.

Having some ideas for what you need to work on written in a disaster plan can be helpful.

At the End of the Competition

Many archers miss the boat after a long day (weekend, week) of competition. They are focused on traveling home, on getting dinner, on starting to think about their real lives (family, school, work, etc.), but there is an advantage lost if within 24 hours of the end of competition you don't take some time to reflect on the experience. I typically ask the competitive archers I am coaching to make two lists within 24 hours of a competition's end: one list is "Things I Learned" and the other is "Things I Would Do Differently Next Time." (Sometimes the first list is "Things I Did Well" but the second list is always the same.) And I want "at least three items" on each list. The requirement of the 24 hours is because we quickly forget small points, especially if we are refocusing on completely different aspects of our lives. The "at least three items" requirement is because we often settle for the easy things, which could be point #1 and point #2, but after you exhaust the things that easily come to mind, you have to reach for something additional, and this is where the really valuable things come from. You know absolutely, that there are things you avoid even talking about because if you do, then you either have to do something or say something you don't want to. But, if you are pursuing excellence in archery, you have to address every aspect of your performance, comfortable or not.

The first topic of your next practice session should be these lists. Is there anything on these lists that you should be working on now because it is more important that what you had planned? I'll give you a clue, if you find something on the "Things I Learned" list that has shown up before on such lists, maybe you ought to pay attention to it. Having to learn a lesson over and over means you are resisting learning that lesson.

Before your next tournament planning session, take a look at the "Things I Would Do Differently Next Time" lists. If you are going to really do anything differently, planning to do things that way is far more effective than making a mental note to, uh, what was it I was going to do? I think you get the idea.

The Bottom Line

I am reiterating this from the planning chapter, but you need a competition plan, which you can write down or not. I recommend that you write it in your performance log as it is too easy to forget what you intend to do when it is not written down. Also, when you write things down they are easier to remember and are seemingly more important than the things you do not write down. This plan needs to include things like: tournament management (checking in, checking scores, rules, judges, tournament directors, etc.), warm-up routine, snacks and meals at the venue, breaks, getting to and back from the venue, sightseeing, equipment checklists, personal items checklists, your "disaster plan," everything.

Why lose because of a simple problem that can be anticipated and solved before it occurs. The saying goes: Persistent Preparation Prevents Poor Performance.

Key Points
Chapter 10 Competing to Win

There is a great deal more to shooting a winning score than: 1. Shoot an X, 2. Repeat.

- What you do *not* want to do is tinker with your equipment, form, or execution just before a competition as there is not enough time to make any such changes into anything but problems.
- You also don't want arduous shooting marathons at this point as you want to be physically and mentally fresh, nor do you want to shoot practice scoring rounds so close to actual competition.
- What you do want to do: you want to rehearse mentally and you want to stay sharp but be relaxed.
- Winners always have pre-competition and competition routines they follow.
- Just before a competition it is helpful to use your imagery skills to place yourself at the venue, in the competition . . . winning.
- Keeping a competition log by taking notes about the venues you compete on can be invaluable. Include in these notes "things you did well" and "things you will do differently next time."
- If you have never been at a particular competition site, ask friends for info, check the Internet. Some information is better than none.
- Create your own warm-up routine and stick with it. The familiarity you have with it will help set you up to have a good competition.
- Having a quiver routine can prevent the mistakes of shooting too many or too few arrows in an end of shooting.
- Arrows have to be inspected each time they are shot.
- Create habits to deal with mistakes you are prone to, like setting your sight twice at each field target if you are inclined to forget to set it to the new dis-

tance to be shot.
- Rules are one thing and courtesy is another. I place courtesy first.
- You need to know the rules of competition, especially those involving equipment failures.
- Having backup gear to replace commonly lost or damaged parts is an absolute necessity. The Roll Royce of backup equipment is a backup bow/setup.
- Managing your competition day is also important, losing because you ran out of energy because you didn't bring food along to eat is a miserable way to learn this lesson. You need to think of everything you might need, could go wrong, or would be useful and plan on it.
- Tournament nerves are normal, as is competition pressure. If these affect you, you need to adopt practices to deal with them.
- The biggest cure for nerves is experience.
- You need a disaster recovery plan, a recovery routine as it were. You also need to make backup goals if you blow off the big ones.

Photo Courtesy of Andy Macdonald

11

Navigating the Archery Organizations

If you are a grizzled veteran of archery competitions, you may want to skip this chapter. Or you may want to read along because I have heard stories from archers about such organizations that I later realized were thirty years old and didn't apply to what was going on now. Archers, especially archers who think they have been mistreated, have very long memories.

Or you may change your mind about becoming a winning archer (at least on a larger scale) and decide to participate in archery as a recreational archer and participate locally. If so, you will probably not get involved with any of the major archery organizations. (There is a list of them below, along with descriptions of their segments of the market.) But, if you decide to compete in archery events with the intent to win them, then you will run up against a general rule in the world of archery: if you want to compete for medals, you must belong to the sponsoring organization. This rule is more than fair. In fact, it would be suicide for any organization to allow otherwise.

If you are happy competing for fun or competing against yourself (trying to better your personal best scores, for example), you may compete in almost any competition as a "Guest." Guests do not get to compete for medals and they often pay a slightly higher entry fee. This is because every archery organization is a collective of archery clubs. Each of these clubs either owns or leases the land upon which their archery range sits and has, beside property taxes or lease payments to make, there are maintenance and other operating expenses to cover. If archers were allowed to compete for medals for just a few extra dollars, there would be no incentive to join the club or the sponsoring organization. Club members do the maintenance and provide the volunteer labor to put on events. The parent organizations exist as rule making bodies, as sponsors for national and international level events, and as recordkeeping bodies. (Ideally, they would also actively promote the sport, but there is only a little of this being done.) Without the "volunteer" labor of their members, archery clubs will go out of existence. This is not just speculation, clubs go out of existence all of the time, some for lack of membership or participation by members. Right now the number of clubs nationally seems to be declining.

I put the word volunteer in quotes above because if you look at the work roster of any club, you will find a small cadre of members who do a huge percentage of the work. Most club members do the minimum number of hours plus a few, but the special members volunteer literally hundreds of additional hours of their labor to keep up the club. Without such "core" members, who are exceedingly generous with their volunteered time, clubs have been known to go out of business. Maintaining an archery range is a great deal of work.

Given all of this, you may wonder why it is that if there is any topic archers are unified behind, it is their antipathy toward archery organizations. Talk to any archer involved in competitive archery and within the first five minutes you will hear a complaint about one of the sponsoring organizations.

In this chapter, I am going to try to explain to you why this is and to offer you some guidance in dealing with the bureaucracy of the sport.

Getting to Know Them

It is time for you to do some research. Introduce yourself to some competing archers and ask them "What do you think is wrong with <insert name of archery organization here>?" Brace yourself for a litany of complaints. If you are inclined to do more than a little research, ask your conversational partners to supply details. (Bring a lawn chair and beverage of choice because you are going to be a while.) Here are the most common complaints:

Poor Communication Every archer I have ever met has mentioned this one. Again, if you are inclined to do any research, check out the websites of the leading archery organizations; here are their web address:

Archery Shooters Association (ASA)
www.asaarchery.com
International Bowhunters Organization (IBO)
www.ibo.net
USA Archery (USAA)/National Archery Association (NAA)
www.usarchery.org
National Field Archery Association (NFAA)
www.nfaa-archery.org

Search their sites for any specific information regarding competition: rules, dress codes, how to get questions answered, names of people in your area who can provide helpful information, lists of coaches available in your area, etc. Think about what it is you might want to know about this sponsoring organization and search for that. Try to find whether your local archery club is listed anywhere. Look for hints and tips about how to participate successfully in archery.

Did you find much? No? Hmm. I wonder what you would get if you telephoned them? (Don't bother, it has been tried.)

Complaints About Costs The next most popular topic to complain about is the cost of everything. One of the wonderful things about the sport of archery is that it is an open sport, meaning there are rarely qualifying scores/events to deal with. If you have been shooting arrows for six months and you think you are ready for the national championships, all you have to do is pay a fee and show up. In fact, if you do go, you will see some of these people on the shooting line. I was once one of those people. At my first national competition I had one goal—to not come in last—and to this day I tell people I came in eighth in my competitive category (from the bottom, I think was 52nd from the top). This is actually way cool! How many other athletes get to compete in their national championships?

But every couple of years, the price of admission goes up and you will hear complaints about how expensive these competitions are (they typically involve travel costs as well). Archers also complain about the cost of dues, mostly I believe because they don't think they are getting value for their money, just frustration. If people were happier with communication, etc., I think there would be far fewer complaints over costs because they really aren't very high at all. If you think organization and club dues in archery are high, check out what is required to join your local golf or tennis club, and you will see that archery fees are quite reasonable. This doesn't change the complaint that people don't feel they are getting their money's worth, and I am not one of the complainers. I am just reporting on what people say.

Confusion Over Rules Rounding out the top three most popular topics to complain about is confusion over the rules.

Some organizations make it simpler. USA Archery uses the rules of it's parent body, the International Archery Federation (formerly FITA, now "World Archery," *www.archery.org*) and you can download their entire rule book from their website. (Much of it concerns international politics, but some sections address the rules of shooting, etc.) This would be wonderful except that USA Archery reserves the right to have additional and/or different rules for competitions. I will not send you on a search for what specifically these rules are as that would be cruel and unusual punishment.

The National Field Archery Association (NFAA) steadfastly refuses to put their rule book online as a free download because they make money selling their rule book. Plus, they change the rules almost every year.

I think you get the point here. But, hey, if you go to the NFAA web site and click on rules, you will not find the rule book for sale. You have to go to "Merchandise" then click on "Miscellaneous" and you will find the "NFAA Constitution & By-Laws" for sale ($8 is quite reasonable). But if you are looking for the NFAA's competition rules, would you look at their "Constitution & By-Laws"? Yeah, neither would I. They don't make it easy.

Outside the "Top Three" There are assorted other complaints about incompetence, for example one of my state archery organizations lost all their archery records and had to beg information from people around the state to reconstitute them, that kind of thing. So is this a story of rampant incompetence, needing revolution to set right? Some think so, but there are reasons for these failings.

There is No "Us," No "Them" Most people think of a national organization and think "big bureaucracy" simultaneously. I am here to tell you that it "ain't so" in archery. Consider USA Archery, the national governing body for Olympic archery. These are the people who put together our Olympic archery teams and World Championship teams (Olympic rules). They have a huge training center at the Olympic Training Center in Chula Vista, CA. They must be big, right?

Wrong.

USA Archery has fewer than a dozen paid employees and a bunch of volunteers; that's it. The Olympic Training Center in Chula Vista is run by the U.S. Olympic Committee (a private organization), not USA Archery, and it supplies the space, support personnel, and room and board for supported athletes and their coaches. The main focus of USA Archery is international competition. But surely they have one person who is solely focused on the base, focused on the next generation of archers. Surely . . . not. They don't have enough people to devote even one position alone to youth archery.

Don't get me wrong, they could do a lot better, they have made a major restructuring effort recently to do just that, but it seems that every time this was done in the past something happened to derail it.

The NFAA, likewise, has few paid employees and a large number of volunteers. Every one of the eight regional councilmen is a volunteer; each of the fifty-one state directors is a volunteer. (That fifty-one is not a typo; the NFAA apparently has a branch operation for Europe. Go figure.) They have a few paid staff and that is it.

I have worked with and for a number of these people (some are friends) and I know they are not bad people. But I also know the outstanding communication issues need to be addressed.

Realize that you are working with pretty much all-volunteer organizations here. The USA Archery judges who spend long hours in the hot sun facilitating fair competition are all volunteers. (Yes, they get a daily stipend for major competitions, and it would be nice if it were big enough to cover their expenses, but it isn't.) Other than the USA Archery's National Coach and his assistant, all USA Archery coaches are volunteers. (I am one, for instance.) I have spent several thousand dollars in travel and training expenses out-of-pocket to be trained as a coach. The NFAA doesn't have as extensive a network of coaches, but theirs aren't paid, either.

Be Part of the Solution If you do get involved in competitive archery, you will have to "deal with" one or more of these organizations, so I am recommending that you keep in mind that most of the people you are talking to are probably volunteers. Cut them a little slack . . . just a little, though. What is needed here is constructive criticism (criticism that doesn't rhyme with witching).

If you have a criticism, share it with the organization, don't just save it up until you have a chance to vent with other archers. (I have sometimes felt that there was a second competition going on during youth championships: the kids vying for medals, and the parents vying for "Best Critical Story Involving an Archery Organization.")

How to Be A Good Complainer Start by being a good participant. If you participate in an archery competition, take the opportunity to thank all of the organizers, judges, etc. Your entry fee did not go straight into their pockets and my experience in untold thousands of hours of volunteer work is that a "thank you" strongly reinforces my inclination to keep volunteering. If there is some small help you can provide, consider offering it. I often come early to events and help set up the archery field, for example, or I help with trash cleanup afterward, that sort of thing. Not only will you get a reputation for being a good person but, if and when you do have a complaint, you will have made it much harder for you to be disregarded.

If you have a complaint, send it on. In this day of email, it costs nothing but a little time to communicate with people. Ask for people's email addresses if they are not posted on the organization's web site; offer your own. If you don't get even a courtesy reply, follow up. Remember that most of the people you are working with are volunteers who have lives of their own.

Connect with other archers, but don't just share stories. Move up a level by asking for suggestions as to how they would "fix" such a problem. Bring in other archers to such a discussion and get their ideas and then pass the best of them on to people who might be able to implement them. Don't assume there are people sitting around in state or national offices brainstorming how to solve problems. (Don't even assume there are offices!) The people in these organizations are closer to the situation described by the old line about "it is hard to focus on draining the swamp when you are up to your "rear" in alligators" than they are to that of think tank bureaucrats.

Join a Club Quite a few competing archers are members of more than one club (currently I am in three and coaching a fourth). Join one. Volunteer your time to maintain one of the ranges we all get to shoot and compete on. Talk to people shooting "Guest" at your club. Ask them to consider becoming members. It is a truism that "many hands make light work."

Don't Complain In Front of the Kids It is easy to fall into the gossip trap; I know as I have repeatedly done so. But if adult archers complain about the archery organizations in front of young archers, attitudes will be formed from something other than those kid's direct experience. Let them enjoy their sport! They can complain later when they become adult archers or archery parents. Your complaints are something your children can't do a thing about, anyway . . . but you can.

Key Points
Chapter 11 Navigating the Archery Organizations

There will always be paperwork and rules. We count on our governing bodies to make these work.

- A fundamental rule is that if you want to compete for medals, you must belong to the sponsoring organization.
- Appreciate the volunteers who run your tournaments. Plain old "thank you's"

go a long way.

- Learn to participate positively to make our archery organizations better. Don't just share your gripes with anyone who will listen.

Sidebar—Archery Organizations, A List

There are a great many archery organizations, most of which go by their initials. Here is a guide to them. Most have websites from which you may be able to get useful information. (Website addresses and phone numbers subject to change.)

ASA (Archery Shooters Association, *www.asaarchery.com*, 770.795.0232) An organization of professional and amateur archers which sponsors unmarked distance 3-D tournaments in the U.S. (simulated hunting scenarios).

ATA (Archery Trade Association) Used to be AMO (Archery Merchants and Manufacturers Association). An independent body claiming to represent archery manufacturers, wholesalers, and retailers. Puts on a massive trade show every January.

FITA (Federation Internationale a Tir a l'Arc/International Archery Federation, *www.archery.org*) Governs Olympic style archery internationally. Sponsors target archery competitions under Olympics and as world and continental championships. You can download their rule book (for free) from their website www.archeryworldcup.org (look under "Rules"). FITA has just changed its name to "World Archery."

IBO (International Bowhunters Organization, *www.ibo.net*, 440.967.2137) An organization of professional and amateur archers which sponsors mostly (unmarked) 3-D competitions in the eastern U.S.

IFAA (International Field Archery Association) Governs field archery internationally. Overlaps with FITA as FITA has a field division. Sponsors target and field archery competitions indoors and out as world and continental championships.

J.O.A.D. (Junior Olympic Archery Development Program, *http://usarchery.org/programs/joad-youth-archery*) USA Archery's youth program. The only archery-only youth program that is reasonably completely developed. This is where the action is in youth competitive teams. Takes teams of Junior and Cadet archers overseas for competition. Has youth only national championships (almost all other organizations allow youths to compete at the same time as adults, but JOAD has "kids only" competitions, the way it should be).

NAA (National Archery Association *aka* USA Archery—see below) Governs Olympic-style archery in U.S. NGB (national governing body) for FITA; also has compound archers who compete up to the FITA world championships, but not in the Olympics. Sponsors target and field archery competitions indoors and out. See USAA.

NADA (National Alliance for the Development of Archery, *www.teacharchery.com*, 352.472.2877) Created to foster the growth of archery in the U.S. Is rapidly becoming the U.S. archery coach's association. Coordinates the training of Level 1 and 2 coaches for the NAA and NFAA as well as for NASP, the Air Force, and other entities. NADA has recently been subsumed into USA Archery.

NASP (National Archery in the Schools Program) A U.S. organization begun in Kentucky and promulgated through state fish and game departments to sponsor short-term archery in PE classes in grammar and high schools. Now in all 50 states and still growing.

NFAA (National Field Archery Association, www.nfaa-archery.org, 605.260.9279) Governs field archery in U.S. NGB (national governing body) for IFAA. Sponsors target, 3-D, and field archery competitions indoors and out.

USAA (USA Archery, *www.usarchery.org*, 719.866.4576) Formerly just the name of that part of the NAA that was the National Governing Body (NGB) or official representative of the U.S. to FITA/World Archery. Recently the NAA has adopted this as the name of the entire organization. USA Archery uses the rules of FITA in its competitions.

Photo Courtesy of Andy Macdonald

12

Competing Internationally

You may want to compete close to home but even that might involve competing internationally (you might live right near a border). Travel restrictions in this age of heightened security complicate matters as does long distance traveling itself. Let's look at this.

Travel

Even if you are traveling with a team sponsored by an archery organization, I recommend that you take full responsibility personally for all of your arrangements. I am not saying that you should make your own arrangements, just that you ask about all arrangements being made for you and be sure you have all of the necessary information. If you miss your flight because you wrote down the time wrong, it is your problem. No matter who makes the mistake that knocks you out of a competition, you suffer. If your travel is sponsored, learn as much as you can from the sponsor, ask a lot of questions. You may get a reputation for being inquisitive, but when you travel without problems, all of the team's coaches will praise you for being a "trouble-free" participant. That can help get you invited back or open up other opportunities for you.

Airport Security Even if you are a seasoned domestic flier, when you travel to other countries, you have to deal with their security systems with which you may be completely unfamiliar. A cooperative attitude goes a long way as does paying attention during team briefings or doing a little Internet research about airport security at your destination before you go. If you try to take your release aid on board, it may get confiscated. A lot of people will take their finger tabs on board. It is highly unlikely that your bow and/or arrows will end up in the cabin with you. It can't hurt to put an explanatory note in your bow case in case it gets inspected. You can't count on baggage inspectors to know what your gear is. There is no excuse for running afoul of airport security with so much information available at your fingertips on the Internet.

Jet Lag and Friends If you are going through more than just a couple of time zones, you will have jet lag to deal with. The general rule is that if your stay is short, try to stay synced to your old time zone. If your stay is more than a couple of days, you will want to get on local time as quickly as possible and the best advice I have heard and tested is to immediately adopt local time. If you land somewhere and it is midnight back where you left, but noon where you are, stay up until your normal bedtime on the local clock, get up in the morning (local time) at your normal hour (local time). This will facilitate your transition being as rapid as possible. If you aren't trying to adapt to local time, you may be competing late in your "night" time or eating dinner early in the morning. This can be more than a little weird, so if you think you can do it, give it a try to see if it works for you.

In some countries drinking water from a tap or fountain is asking for a case a diarrhea which can knock you right out of a competition. Be sure you know whether you can "drink the water" at your destination. Another consideration is food. If the tournament site is known worldwide for its sea food and you are allergic or just really don't like fish, etc. you have to do some research to determine what local food you can eat. One option is, if you have a unit you can cook in, that you cook your own food. You will have to schedule time for shopping, cooking, and cleaning up. You will need enough local currency, transportation to and from stores, etc. Think about what you will be doing to see if you will have the time. Sponsored team events often provide itineraries that should enable you to plan your time well. Do realize that if you take the attitude that you will only eat at MacDonald's, you will get a reputation and it won't be a flattering one. Host countries want to see you tasting their culture and food is part of that.

Even people with cast iron stomachs (who can eat anything) have been known for taking "comfort foods" along with them. This may be candy bars, dried fruit, nuts, MoonPies, etc., foods that say "home" to them. Such foods can be calming when you get anxious about being away from home, or when being in a country whose language you don't speak and your level of confusion gets incapacitating.

Performance Enhancing Drugs

If you do go overseas to compete, you will find that more than a few countries take archery very seriously, more seriously than we do by far. Sanctioned international archery events are often treated like ordinary sporting events, including drug testing. I won't say anything about taking recreational drugs in a foreign country except that you may be taking chances you can't possibly evaluate, which is stupid, but "ordinary" medications, even prescribed medications, or "over the counter" dietary supplements can get you disqualified.

You can get the current "banned substances" list from the World Anti-Doping Agency (WADA, *www.wada-ama.org/en/*) which you then need to read very carefully. Realize that every pharmaceutical company who puts out a drug gives its own brand name. Vitamin C has over 200 names associated with it (the vast majority are for marketing purposes). You need to look for the scientific names (and any of the other names) for medicines you take on these lists. If you are unsure you can ask WADA.

As another example, a very small number of sports have banned alcohol (archery is one of them!) as something that can enhance performance by calming nerves. Other sports haven't gotten around to it or bothered because there is no benefit that affects performance in their sport. Most people wouldn't think of alcohol as a drug, but if you have beer or wine for lunch on the day of a competition and get tested, you may not pass the test.

There are quite a few ordinary prescription medicines on these lists, so if you are taking them, you need to let your team know, or ask the sponsoring organization. Or ask WADA. More information can also be had from the U.S. Anti-Doping Agency (USADA, *www.usantidoping.org*).

Key Points
Chapter 12 Competing Internationally

There are a whole new set of challenges when competing internationally. One is the possibility of drug testing.

- International travel sometimes includes vastly different security schemes. Be prepared; do some research.
- Jet lag has to be considered for you to have a good tournament.
- Food and drink in foreign countries can be sources of disease and discomfort that can cost you your competitive edge.
- Common medications, even mild alcohol consumption, can get you disqualified from competition. Get fully informed before you leave.

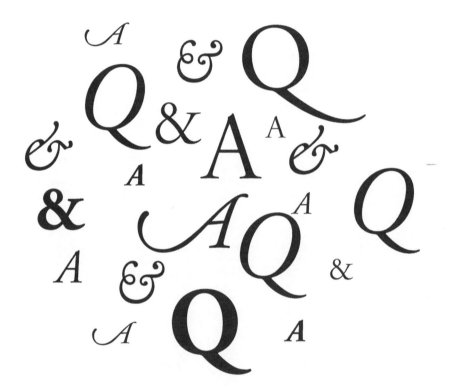

Questions and Answers

Here are some questions and answers that may address some of the things I didn't cover, or didn't cover in enough detail above.

Form and Execution

Q Why don't we want to grip the bow in a "pistol grip" or tightly?

A Because tight hand muscles create variation in the shot. If the muscles are very tight, the bow recoils off the surface quite a bit. If the hand is loose, it recoils only a bit. If more than one muscle group is involved, the bow will jump left and right based on differences in tension in those muscles. Even after being instructed, beginners tend to grip their bows too tightly. Subconsciously they don't want to drop their bow, which they will if they shoot it the way we tell them to. A "pistol grip" brings more muscles (that may get tense) into contact with the bow.

Q So what does a sling do?

A It teaches your subconscious mind that there is no need to "grab the bow" upon release, because the bow can't be dropped. When I introduce slings, I ask my students to put on the sling, hold their bow at arm's length, and drop it! "The sling prevents the bow from falling, see?"

Q So, what if I don't want to use a sling?

A Then you will be grabbing the bow after each shot. The danger is: shoot-grab, shoot-grab, shoot-grab can become shoot-grab, shoot-grab, grab-shoot (Ooooops!).

Q But the Olympic Gold Medalist ...

A Uh hunh! I watched videos of his performance very carefully and after every shot in which I could see his bow hand, his fingertips turned white. In other words, he was grabbing his bow. Apparently the cost of doing this is not so much that you can't win an Olympic Gold Medal.

The big point here, is there is not necessarily an advantage in not using a sling of some kind. Mr. Ruban trained himself so that there was no disadvantage. I can see no advantage from not using a sling, so I still recommend them. And there is a training cost to not using a sling. You have to train yourself to not grab the bow out of order, but then you have to train yourself to use a sling, too.

Equipment

Q I am really confused. There are so many options for equipment, how do I make good decisions?

A If you asked yourself this question, you have had a breakthrough! First, here is a list of things not to do:
• switch something because of an advertisement
• switch something because of the recommendation of a shop
• switch something because of the recommendation of a buddy
• switch something because of the recommendation of a book
• switch something because of the recommendation of a magazine article
• switch something because of the casual recommendation of an expert archer or coach.

Are you seeing the pattern here? All of these sources of advice are available to you and valuable for suggestions of things to try, but they don't constitute reasons to use some new piece of archery gear.

Here are a list of things to consider when addressing new archery gear:
• Am I unhappy with the performance of my current gear? (If so, why?)
• Is this a good time to change anything?
• If I make this switch, how many points is it worth?

At one point I was unhappy with my stabilizer. Even though I had no real evidence, I felt like my old stabilizer was the real cause of being blown off targets by gusting winds. So, I changed from a tube stabilizer to a multi-rod stabilizer and I have less trouble with the wind now, but do I really *know* the stabilizer change was the cause? Probably not. Actually, since I don't have a problem right now, I don't need to address the issue, so I don't.

Q I am thinking of making the switch from X Brand aluminum/carbon arrows to Y Brand all-carbon arrows. Is this a good idea?

A What you are asking is: how much is this change worth to me? This is a very important question, but one also very difficult to answer. Imagine what the world would be like if there were exact ways to evaluate equipment expressed as increased performance in a standard round. "Elite archers increased their NFAA Field Round scores by 0.7%!" or "FITA Round score improvements of three points have been validated." This would be an advertiser's nightmare—instead they want you to use your imagination so that, in your mind, switching to a new super, duper release aid will increase your 300 round score by 30%! In reality, most accomplished archers can shoot very good scores with quite modest equipment. The first time I shot a "perfect" NFAA Indoor Round of 300/300 I was using a 10 year old bow with older Easton ACC arrows. This was actually an outdoor setup as I hadn't gotten an indoor bow ready. I only got 42 of a possible 60 X's so it was far from perfect, but how is anyone going to sell me on the idea that I can make a significant score improvement with some new piece of gear. To a very (very!) large extent, especially indoors, it is the archer, not the equipment which is responsible for the score.

Q A buddy is recommending that I get a <fill in the blank>. What do you think?

A If your equipment limits your performance in some way (your sight gets loose frequently and slips to a different, lower setting or your arrows aren't all the same weight or spine, or . . . or . . .) then fixing it or replacing it will make an immediate improvement in performance. In my opinion, the source of most casual recommendations is, well, for example:

Archer A: "Wow, these XYZ carbons shoot better than any other arrow on the market!"

You: "Uh, what were you shooting before?"

Archer A: "Oh, I shot arrows I made from wood dowels."

This was intended to be funny, but many "casual recommendations" you will get from other archers are about equally based on realistic comparisons. The reason I can say this confidently is because it is so hard to make valid comparisons that most people won't do the work.

On the other hand, I knew a professional archer who had walked away from his long time bow sponsor to a new sponsor. He was given a new bow which he proceeded to set up and tune. He then shot several test rounds. The results were disappointing, so he tried a different tune. The next several test rounds also had disappointing results. So, he got out his old bow and shot with it. His scores and X counts were right on what they used to be, so he then knew it wasn't him. Since these were indoor rounds, it wasn't the wind or the sun, either. He contacted the technical reps of the company for advice. He contacted other archers on setting up and tuning that model of bow. In the end he had shot almost forty 300 point Vegas Rounds and his average score was lower by a little over 1 point and his X count was 2-3 less per round. In the end, he contacted his new company rep and his old one and the new one let him out of his contract and his old one took him back. I tell you this as an example of the manufacturer's reps and the archer all doing what was right. (You will hear "horror stories" from other archers and maybe this will balance some of those out.) The main point here is the archer, who was a pro but archery wasn't his full-time job, shot dozens and dozens of rounds, tried various setups and tunes, talked to service reps and other archers to make sure he wasn't doing anything wrong. All of this to evaluate a bow. This is not something most archers will do. Their opinions are based on far, far less effort, in general. So, if somebody gives you a great recommendation for a piece of archery gear, ask them how do they know it is "great" or "the best." Ask them "How many other arrows, or release aids, or whatever did they compare the recommended one to?"

 At a recent tournament I had to replace my bowstring and it threw everything off. Any suggestions?

 A top professional archer and coach showed me a useful practice which I now recommend to you. He buys a bow square for every bow he owns. The bow square has pieces of tape on it where he has marked things like the locations of his nock locators, and his brace height (front and back of the string), and his tiller measurements, when the bow square is placed properly to check those things. He said "Why have to read a scale and remember a number (and whether you measure brace height to the front, center, or back of the string) when you can just put marks on the tape where those things are supposed to be?" Good advice. He also put a bigger piece of tape on the side not used (the metric side if there is one and you are from the U.S.) and he wrote all of the important measurements for that bow (axle-to-axle, peep to nocking point distance, cable and bow string lengths, etc.). In addition, his bow was marked as to the positions of the arrow rest, bow sight extension length, positions of the eccentrics at brace ... everything. If anything on that bow were to break or move, it or a replacement could be fitted almost exactly in very short order, without having to retune the bow. Another good approach is the "short arrow technique" which you can read about in "The Short Arrow Technique" by Tom Dorigatti in Vol. 13, No. 4 of *Archery Focus* magazine.

Steve Ruis

Appendices

Additional Resources

There are many fine books and DVDs on various topics you need to learn about. Here are some which I can highly recommend.

Resources for Everyone

Simple Maintenance for Archery
by Alan Anderson and Ruth Rowe

There is a great little book that has step-by-step instructions (with photos) on how to do almost all maintenance on your bow and arrows. It is highly recommended, in fact, all archers need a copy of this book.

Easton Arrow Tuning and Maintenance Guide
by Easton Archery

Easton Archery makes the vast majority of aluminum, carbon, and aluminum-carbon arrow shafts in the world. This tuning guide is a free download (from all over the place as well as the AER website). It has come out in a number of editions, the earlier editions are more appropriate for what we are doing (the most recent goes into the tuning of $400/dozen Olympic arrows). This guide covers all of the aspects of how to select arrow shafts, build arrows, and tune them. Highly recommended resource.

Resources for Olympic-Style Archers

Fundamentals of Recurve Target Archery
by Ruth Rowe

Ruth Rowe covers all of the basics of shooting Olympic-style from a coach's vantage point. This book is not as comprehensive as "The Simple Art of Winning," but maybe not as overwhelming, either.

Handbook of Modern Recurve Tuning
by Richard A. Cockrell

This is a step-by-step guide to tuning recurve bows. Is designed to be used as a reference and includes a set of instructions for each task.

The Simple Art of Winning
by Rick McKinney

This is the "bible" of Olympic-style archery (American-style). Written by a three-time World Champion and two-time Olympic silver medalist.

Total Archery/Total Archery: Inside the Archer
by KiSik Lee

KiSik Lee is one of the most successful Olympic archery coaches and is currently USA Archery's National Head Coach. He has put a wealth of information into these two books and you may need a very high level coach or one trained by Coach Lee to help you put that information to work.

Archery: The Art of Repetition
by Simon S. Needham

Now in paperback this book joins McKinney's and Lee's as all-in-one references on Olympic-style archery. There is also a really cool companion DVD that offers one of the best O-style recurve bow setup demonstrations I have seen.

Resources for Compound Archers

Compound archery is the most popular form of archery in the U.S. But because compound bows use mechanical advantage to launch arrows, tuning and adjusting them is a much more mechanical process, so these books are a bit more "engineery" than the others.

Tuning Your Compound Bow, 4th Ed.
by Larry Wise

Compound bows are mechanical contraptions and professional archer, coach, and bow mechanic Larry Wise walks you though all of the details. Covers bows (all styles of compounds) and arrows. Will be intimidating to those new to compound bows, but start by skimming to find the basics and skip over the more complicated bits.

Core Archery
by Larry Wise

This little book not only covers compound bow shooting form but all of the biomechanical reasons for why we shoot them they way we do. There is no better book on compound bow shooting form and execution.

Resources for the Mental Game

The mental game is crucial to becoming a consistent performer and, hence, a consistent winner. Here are two absolute "must have" resources.

With Winning in Mind
by Lanny Bassham

There is no better place to start to learn about the mental game of archery (even though the author was a rifle marksman). This little book has sold over 100,000 copies to archers, golfers, dog agility trainers, and beauty pageant competitors. Obviously its contents have application to more things than archery. Highly recommended.

Mental Keys that Unlock Target Panic, Parts 1 & 2
by Len Cardinale

These videos, by one of the founders of the mental game for archery, are absolute "must sees".

Miscellaneous Resources

- *Easton Archery Spine Chart* (available online from Easton Archery Products, *www.eastonarchery.com*, look under "Company" then "Downloads")
- *FITA Rule Book* The FITA Rule Book (used by USA Archery) and much more is available at www.archery.org. Look under "Rules" and "Publications."
- *NFAA Constitution and Rules* Should be free, but its not. (republished every year by the NFAA, *www.fieldarchery.org*)
- *The Heretic Archer* by Vittorio and Michele Frangilli
  This book combined with McKinney's and Lee/deBondt's constitute a complete library on Olympic-style archery.
- *Idiot Proof Archery* by Bernie Pellerite
  An omnibus on everything compound (available from *www.robinhoodvideos.com*).
- *Professional Archery Technique* by Kirk Etheridge, 3rd Ed.
  This was the first book to describe the framing techniques then being used illegally in unmarked distance competitions. Addresses compound bows only (available at many bookstores and online).
- ⊙ *Straight Talk from the Pros* (by Carter Enterprises)
  Not only for the release aid advice but advice along the way on shooting form and winning from top compound archers, this is a must view video (available from *www.carterenterprises.com*).
- *Mastering Bow Tuning* by James Park
  Australian James Park has written a number of books like this one which came out first on CD for easy distribution (not easy to find, though).

In several places in this book I have recommended resources that are available with a subscription to *Archery Focus* magazine. As examples of articles that could be helpful to you I compiled this short list:

Video as a Training Tool by Mark Lonsdale (Vol 6, No. 1) Everything you need to know about how to videotape yourself.

Aiming and Sighting by Larry Wise (Vol 5 No 5)

Assessment by Alison Rhodius (Vol 6, No. 6)

Comfort Zones by Lisa Franseen, Ph.D. (Vol 4, No. 6)

Does Positive Self-talk Really Work? by Lisa Franseen, Ph.D. (Vol 5, No. 6)

Don't Keep a Diary, Keep a Performance Journal by Lanny Bassham (Vol 9, No. 1)

Goal Setting–Process or Outcome? by Lanny Bassham (Vol 8, No. 1)

How to Level Your Compound Bow Sight by Gene Lueck (Vol 6 No 4) All you need to set all three axes on a bow sight are demonstrated.

Make Your Own Ethafoam™ Targets by Ty Pelfrey (Vol 7 No 3) Want targets you can lug around? Here's how to make them.

Making Your Students Mentally Tough by Lisa Franseen, Ph.D. (Vol 4, No. 1&2)

Perfect Sight Tapes for Your Target Bow by Steve Ruis (Vol 8 No 2) Once you've printed out a beautiful computer-generated sight tape, how to put it on the bow and make it weatherproof.

Pressure–Is It Friend or Foe? by Lanny Bassham (Vol 7, No. 2)

Rain . . . I Hate Rain! by Karl A. Stolleis (Vol 4 No 3) All about rain gear and how to use it.

Shooting FITA Field Unmarked Distances by Tim Mundon (Vol 6, No 3) This article describes distance estimating/ranging techniques for unmarked yardage shots.

Shooting in the Wind and Rain by Bernie Pellerite (Vol 4 No 2)

Stop the Sun, Not the Fun! by Pedro Serraheiro (Vol 4 No 5) How to prevent overexposure to the sun and what to do when it happens.

Target Panic!!! by Lisa Franseen, Ph.D. (Vol 5, No. 3)

The 7 Habits of Successful Olympic Round Shooters by Lloyd Brown (Vol 2 No 5)

The Importance of Practice Sessions That Have a Plan by Mike Gerard (Vol 3 No 4)

The Very Last Word on Shooting Up and Down Hill by Steve Ruis (Vol 3 No 5) There is plenty more that could be said, but this is a good start.

Visualization by Lisa Franseen, Ph.D. (Vol 1, No. 5 and Vol 2, No. 1)

Why Does Canting Work? by Aaron Stone (Vol 7 No 4)

Why You Need to Use a D-Loop by George Chapman (Vol 7, No. 5) Master Coach George Chapman explains the whys of using a D-loop on your compound bow before showing you the simplest and most secure way of tying one on.

Notes

Notes

Finally, A Book On Coaching Archery!

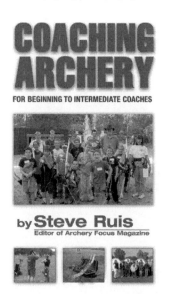

There are lots of books about archery—about archery form, archery execution, archery equipment, even archery history; but there weren't any books in print on archery coaching . . . until now. Finally there is a book on coaching for beginning to intermediate archery coaches. In **Coaching Archery** you will learn not *what* to teach (which you can get from those other books) but *how* to teach it and much more you won't get from certification courses. Topics include:

- tips on running programs
- the styles of archery
- the mental side of archery
- an exploration of archery coaching styles
- helping with equipment
- coaching at tournaments
- plus, advice on becoming a better coach from some top coaches

There are even seven whole pages of resources for coaches! If you are a archery coach looking to increase your coaching skills, this is the book for you!

128 pages • ISBN 978-0-9821471-0-8 • US $19.95

Available at Better Bookstores and Online

Made in the USA
Charleston, SC
08 August 2012